"Stacey Canfield has done [...] can provide love and care [...] the Soul Sitter. Not only will this book help the ordinary person facing the death of a loved one, but also professional care-givers. She has a unique story to tell, plus provides useful insights that will encourage many people. I wholeheartedly recommend it!"

— *George Pratt, PhD*
Past Chairman of Psychology, Scripps Memorial Hospital, La Jolla, California; coauthor: *Instant Emotional Healing: Acupressure for the Emotions; A Clinical Hypnosis Primer; and Hyper-Performance: Release Your Business Potential*

"I met Stacey Canfield after my own journey as a Soul Sitter ended. Being a caregiver and soul sitter for my husband of 36 years changed my life forever. Meeting Stacey was a positive force and she invited me in to join her mission. As a long time volunteer for hospice, I invited her on a tour. She immediately became a big supporter of hospice. Her invitation to write for SoulSitter.com was a powerful catharsis for me. Stacey's book provides an avenue for those soul sitting and caring for the dying to embrace the experience for themselves while ensuring a quality of life while dying for those facing the reality of death."

—*Linda Strause, PhD*
Executive Director and Head, Clinical Operations, Vical Inc., Research Scholar & Founding Research Ethics Chair for San Diego Hospice and Institute for Palliative Medicine, and Adjunct Prof. UCSD Dept. Biology

"It is inevitable…we will all die. Until now the conversation for families, friends and individuals supporting loved ones in transition has been largely unspoken. Stacey Canfield in her remarkable and ground breaking book "The Soul Sitter" explores the power behind the conversation to break this silence. In doing so she moves you to new insights about yourself, family, friends and the power of love in death."

— *Dr Sarah Farrant, DC, BSc, Grad Dip Psych, B Phys Ed.* Chiropractor, Award Winning Author, International Speaker, "Mother of Vitalism." Author of *The Vital Truth*®: *Accessing The Possibilities of Unlimited Health*

"Stacey Canfield has pulled together a profound set of desperately needed tools to empower anyone through the life transition we call death. If you are ready to make a positive difference in the world then read through this book and apply this unique recipe of love to those around you. I have been a Psychotherapist for nearly 30 years, and I believe Stacey's message is vital to all of us making a healthy and loving transition. The mission of Soul Sitters is more than a method, it is a movement from fear to love."

—*Sara G. Gilman, M.F.T., F.A.A.E.T.S* Marriage & Family Therapist, Fellow, American Academy of Experts in Traumatic Stress, EMDR Approved Consultant

# The Soul Sitter's Handbook

What to do when your loved one is dying

# The Soul Sitter's Handbook

What to do when your loved one is dying

## Stacey Canfield

With Candace George Conradi

*Anastacia Media Group*

# The Soul Sitter's Handbook
What to do when your loved one is dying

**Cataloging in Publication Data**
Canfield, Stacey
The Soul Sitter's Handbook/ Stacey Canfield—[1st ed.]
        p. cm.
ISBN: 978-0-9829576-1-5
1. Grief  2. Loss  3. Soul care    I. Title    II. Author
BF575.C1626 2011      155.9'37—dc22

ISBN: 978-0-9829576-1-5

**To my amazingly supportive husband, Daniel.**

Thank you for embracing my vision when
I returned from Miraval. You are truly my
divine compliment.

# Contents

# Foreword

## *by Brenda Strong*

*The dearly departed narrator Mary Alice Young on*
*Desperate Housewives*

People think I know all about the mysteries of life and death because of my role as Mary Alice Young on the TV show, *Desperate Housewives*. I play the dearly departed neighbor in an ensemble that includes Marcia Cross, Teri Hatcher, Felicity Huffman, Eva Longoria, and other gifted cast members, including previous season regulars, Nicolette Sheridan and Dana Delany. My voice from beyond the grave escorts the viewer from week to week, revealing the moral themes of the show, which are written beautifully by the show's creator, Marc Cherry.

Even though I am "in" every episode, I physically appear primarily in flashbacks at this point. In season one my character committed the desperate act of suicide after doing something she had to do to protect her family.

Since that first season, I have been the ethereal voice who directs and interprets the lives of the women of Wisteria Lane. I have the privilege of being rather omniscient, and that leads to confusion in the minds of some fans of the show that believe I have clairvoyant powers. I wish I did, but I don't. I struggle with issues of life and death just like everyone else.

Desperate Housewives has been a thrill. The producers say we have 120 million worldwide viewers, and I'm glad we are able to bring joy to so many people.

In my real life, I find that yoga helps me better understand others, the Universe and myself. It centers me, helps relax my body, reduces stress, and enhances blood and energy flow. All of these things provide me with an inner harmony that enables me to live a very busy life. Yoga enhances spirituality too. A healthy body in proper posture has the power to receive all the Universe has to offer.

Because of my beliefs about the great healing power of the Universe, it was no surprise that Stacey Canfield came back into my life at a very remarkable time. We exchanged emails just a day after my dad Jason died, and I was feeling a deep sense of loss.

Stacey told me about the calling she had, to help people better understand how they could remain present and caring as a loved one experiences their final hours. She had created a web site, www.SoulSitters.com, which is filled with helpful and inspiring information about reaching out to others as they prepare to exit this world.

After watching my mother suffer through a debilitating stroke for 15 years prior to her death, having lost my brother in his 30's to a brain tumor, and knowing countless friends who were dealing with loss and illness of loved ones, I knew that the message of "Soul Sitting" was timely. It is a needed voice for all to hear, one that helps people understand how they can gracefully accept life's inevitable transition.

I was moved beyond belief by Stacey's story. Now, you have to understand, I had to wrap my brain around the fact that sitting opposite of me was a beautiful woman of wisdom. After all, I first met Stacey when she was just twelve years old. I was dating her brother Scott while I was a student at Arizona State University. I was a Musical Theatre major there and was Miss Arizona, and was busy competing in the Miss America competition. It was a fun time for me, and I enjoyed meeting Scott's family on a vacation to San Diego.

After I learned of Stacey's mission, we met and had an amazing time together. Not only did I learn of her love of yoga, but I was also able to hear the remarkable story that you will read here. As her story unfolded, I could see that her vision of Soul Sitting would be her gift to the world.

Stacey and I shared a few tears together at that meeting as we shared loving stories about our departed fathers. Stacey is an extremely compassionate person, and I was reminded again that suffering can be turned into blessing when we unite our souls with the Universe.

You will enjoy Stacey's story. Not only does she reveal practical techniques for caring for the dying, but she also reveals her own soul. She describes her struggles and experiences in a very inspiring way. Let's face it— we all could use a guide from "beyond" to escort us through the complexities of life, like Mary Alice does on Desperate Housewives. You will be able to face matters of life and death from a new perspective after you read The Soul Sitter.

**Brenda Strong**
Hollywood, California

# Acknowledgments from Stacey

So many people influenced this work. I offer my homage to Dr. Elisabeth Kübler-Ross for the five stages of grief and loss she formulated. She opened up the door of conversation around death in her work and eventual book, On Death and Dying. Her brilliance and courage helped many conquer the fears and taboos of this life process. Her work became the principles for the foundation of the Three Triads. My homage would not be complete without acknowledging and offering my gratitude to David Kessler for continuing and expanding the understanding first established in Dr. Kübler-Ross's work.

I would like to acknowledge the work of Dr. Brian Weiss who opened up a vista of healing and understanding of the death process for me. Through his work, I came to understand that death comes in many forms in our lives — through endings that we all face. Those endings come through divorce, job loss, home loss, relationships that break down — all aspects of "death" that I had never labeled in that way. He also helped me consider the mysteries of death that offered solace and understanding.

I would like to thank the "professional" soul sitter Sara Gilman, whose life and work inspires me every day. For over a decade, she has been more than a friend to me; she has been my cheerleader, coach and confidante. It was Sara who introduced me to my most cherished new friend, Linda Strause, who presented me to all of the amazing people at San Diego Hospice and the Institute for Palliative Medicine.

A huge group-hug goes to Lisa Sasevich and all the "Sassy Mastermind" women for giving me a reason to drive to the desert and find the sacred oasis that is the Miraval. Thank you to all of the strong angels of encouragement who watched me climb a thirty-five foot pole and leap off with no fear. My life changed that weekend, and I am so glad they were all there supporting me along the way.

I must thank Daniel—my husband. I'm grateful he did not hang up on me when I called at midnight from my Miraval suite to ask him a profound question : "Are you ready for our life to change?" He could have easily said, "No, I'm comfortable with things as they are," and fought me the whole way. Instead, his love reached through the phone and embraced me with trust and reassurance. "Yes, honey," he said. "I'm ready."

I am eternally grateful to Ms. Tina Powers for unlocking the mission that would become Soul Sitters. Our first meeting was extraordinary. I knew right away that we would be friends for life.

Amethyst Wyldfyre saw something in me, something much bigger than what and who I am. She had the true vision of what was to come. She inspired me to go forward with this work. I soulfully thank her for putting me on Mother Nature's path of strength and truth; for opening my eyes to the intense beauty of life. I will never look at anything the same from having known her.

To my dear mother, Patricia, who has always believed in me no matter how intense my dreams and ideas may have been. Her love and support through all my challenges and triumphs buoys my courage and my soul. Thank you for our many hour-long phone conversations and for supporting my embryonic ideas. It was your faith in me that helped me to birth Soul Sitters. I love you Momma-cita!

I can't forget my brothers, sisters and extended family who were so open to hear my story. Thank you for listening unconditionally and offering loving support, even when you didn't understand the whole purpose.

A warm embrace goes out to Brenda Strong. I will never forget how she held my hands encouraging me to speak my truth and not be attached to fear as we stood in her dining room. Thank you for lighting potential new paths to help heal the world.

I want to thank the persons who technically made this book possible. First, Donald L. Hughes, who saw there was a book in my story. Gratitude also extends to Candace Conradi, who became the architect of my voice, giving it shape and foundation. Finally, Christine Sullivan, our patient proofreader and sounding board. A sincere thank you to Beverly Bergman, a trusted friend and talented editor who helped make *Soul Sitters* clear and precise. And finally, to Diane Salucci, who did one last proof for accuracy of content and changes. It has taken a village of dedicated individuals to bring it to fruition. I am indebted to you all.

A final thank you to my upstairs team—the male guardians who watch over me: Vince, Jerry, Richard, Fred, and my beautiful father, Chuck. These strong men still serve as vital influences in my life. I think of them often and am proud to pass on their legacy of love and spirit.

Finally, with deepest gratitude, I thank my tribe of mother figures, those I lovingly refer to as my Mother Guides: Grandma Ingeborg; my mother-in-law Edna; my Godmother Mary; and my maternal grandmother, Grandy. These are the women for whom I provided soul care. An image of them taking their last breaths is with me every day, and it motivates me to pass along their grace and wisdom. It is the soul sitting stories of these four women that I feel compelled to reveal in this book. I look forward to introducing you to each of their lovely spirits and light.

The spiritual discoveries I experienced with my Mother Guides in their last moments of life on earth planted the seed for this book. In their honor, I move forward on my mission to provide a path for others on how to live after letting go.

*Stacey Canfield*

# Introduction

There is no simple formula for processing what is before you, when faced with the imminent death of a loved one. I know this with all certainty. My intention for writing this book begins and ends with a deeply seeded desire not only to ease your pain, but to somehow lessen the chaos that can appear under stress. I want to acknowledge that death feels unfair and we are often left questioning the very nature of life itself. In the depth of sorrow, most of us feel alone, even if we are surrounded by people we love. Since my work began in this field, ironic as it may sound, loneliness seems to be the common thread that binds us together. Most everyone, including myself, reaches a point when there is a feeling that no one else on the planet has ever felt the depth of sorrow we are feeling. Certainly, to lose someone we love to death may be the single greatest mystery of life and the hardest one to accept. But it is also a part of life. Death of a loved one is something we must all face, sooner or later. I faced it far sooner than I ever expected I would. But before I share that with you, I want to share a few other things about me.

For as long as I can remember, I have felt a kinship to my spirituality. When I was young, my faith was established as a member of the Catholic Church, the religion of my family. As

I reflect on that early influence, I have come to treasure the sacred training I received at the hands of those who taught me. I attended an all-girls' Catholic high school and, because there were no males to compete with, I learned the value of my strength as a woman and a leader. In this safe culture, I found my self-assurance and my deep abiding faith in God.

At one point, as a high school student in my senior year, I chose an elective class entitled "Life and Its Beyond." It was taught by Carole Slacks, an energetic and insightful young woman in her twenties. Our class assignment was to plan our personal funeral and bequeath our legacy and belongings to people we loved. Needless to say, as impressionable young women, not only I, but all my classmates were deeply moved. The shared experience wove us together into a sisterhood and closeness I had never felt before. It was truly a life changing experience for all of us.

During that same year, I elected to take a class on Comparative Religions of the world. In some ways, this concept seemed contradictory to the rules and guidelines set forth by my Catholic faith. As I matured, I discovered that some of the most insightful teachers within Catholic education are the willing spiritual explorers, seeking to understand the mysticism of faith and God's relationship to us as human beings. The ideas and concepts I learned in my Comparative Religion class opened me to a world of possibilities for my spirituality, never excluding the mystical and transformative message of Jesus, the Christ.

Beginning with that experience, and many experiences I have had since that time, death has always been in my radar. Because I do not believe in accidents or coincidence, I realize there were no mistakes in my early religious training or in the choice of classes I took my senior year. Catholicism and the discipline of religious practice deeply rooted me to the innate mysticism of my relationship with God. The ceremony and practices grounded me and taught me the importance of ritual. I have come to know that ritual is our phone call to that loving energy that waits patiently for our attention. Now, as an adult, I find myself in daily conversation with that Eternal Being who I sometimes refer to as God and other times Source or the Universe. In essence, I feel words fade when trying to describe the essence of so great a Being.

I am quite certain my early life experiences of losing five of my family members has prepared me for my work with *Soul Sitters*. All my experiences culminated during a fateful weekend in January 2010, while driving through the desert. Up until then, my life had been somewhat ordinary, focused around my work and my family. But on a Friday morning, in the middle of the Arizona desert, my life changed. One moment, I was a photographer and artist, hired to take pictures at a women's retreat — and in the next moment (and the moments that followed), my life shifted in ways I could never have expected. Soul Sitters was founded and within 108 days a website was created, offering solace to those facing the death of their loved ones.

I do not label myself as an expert; I have not been classically trained in the sciences or in psychology; I am not a religious scholar. But the insights and guidance I have received in the past two years continue to speak to me clearly and persistently, guiding me and inspiring me in my work.

I am driven in a very rooted and peaceful way to serve others. The information in this handbook comes not only from my inspiration, but is a collaborative work in many ways. The one thing I know with all certainty is that it is time to reopen the conversation in our culture around death and dying. I hope those who read this book will be touched and motivated to respond in new and encouraging ways when faced with the uncertainties and suffering of personal loss. My love goes out to all, and I pray you receive many gifts from these pages.

In *The Soul Sitter's Handbook* I delve into the practical aspects of caring for the dying. The various tools in the following pages were received on the wings of inspiration and prayer that evolved into the ideas and practical suggestions that I share with you. I feel each suggestion, from the *The Steps*, to the *Positive Grief Method*, to the *Triads of Soul Care*, is practical and easily implemented. They apply across the board for anyone seeking ways to be more comfortably and peacefully present with the dying. Quite honestly, I have found them effective in my everyday life and they have often made a profound difference in my relationships with those who live on as well.

The glossary also includes a reading list that has been compiled for those wishing to explore the nature of living and dying. The books lend themselves to the theme of life being eternal in nature. The list will be provided on the *www.SoulSitter. com* website. If you have discovered reference material that has helped you, we invite you to share those books, tools, and ideas on our site as well. Our goal is to provide a resource for those seeking guidance. As the founder of Soul Sitters, I learn every day the importance of examining my own thought patterns and beliefs. I realize now how limiting some of those perspectives have been. As difficult as change has been, I humbly acknowledge that my willingness to change my mind has expanded my life and given my lungs a little more room to breathe. I honestly do not know the future of Soul Sitters or where this will all lead. What I am quite certain of is that this message fell into my hands and it is up to me to share it with others. It was soulfully necessary for me to follow the new path set before me. I am, quite simply, deeply grateful. It is an honor to join the many voices who are working to change our language and our views around life and death.

Soul Sitters changed my life forever and I am hopeful that it will also change your life in some positive way.

**Soul Sitter** (sohl-sit-er) **n.**

1. A person who is present at the final passing of a loved one.

2. A person or group of people who are present for the journey of someone's terminal illness.

# Chapter One
# When Death Meets Life

*All water has a perfect memory and is trying to*
*get back to where it was.*

TONI MORRISON

I want you to take a deep breath and repeat the word aloud with me. If it helps, pretend someone is there with you, saying it at the same time.

Say the word "death."

Say it again and take a breath.

Now, one more time, say it again and take another breath.

Notice nothing bad happened as you said the word. Perhaps you felt a release in saying it; or your heart might have raced and your palms may have become sweaty. But in this moment, right where you are sitting, notice nothing has changed…except perhaps your perception. The wind still blew, the sun still shone (or the moon still sat adrift in the sky). Acknowledging "death" did not stop the planet from spinning or the clock from ticking.

At some point in my journey of life, I realized that **not** saying the word "death" aloud did nothing to delay or prevent it from coming. To never utter the syllable did not hold death at bay. But

1

when I had the courage to say it aloud, it became less scary to me. It did not stop my sorrow; it simply made it more real. And while my heart might have been breaking, when I acknowledged "death" for what it was, I felt more alive. I was no longer cutting myself off from my life. I accepted, in that moment, that death happens.

Giving tone to this word will give value to your life. In truth, we are all the same. I am no different from you or your neighbor, or your best friend, or the homeless person on the street. We all, each of us, to the last person on this planet, have this one thing in common. We must all meet death.

As a young girl, I wished for fairytale experiences and could see no downside to my blissful existence. In my mind, there was no potential for sadness. But like everyone, growing up is inevitable and at some point along the way I had to accept the truth about Santa Claus and the Easter Bunny. But those shocking truths were always shared with my peers as our fairy tales simultaneously combusted into fact. For most of us who live in safety, with shelter, food, and clothing, this is simply part of our childhood. I gave up those small fantasies without too much trauma, taking with stride the facts of life that continually floated to the surface.

My early life was secure. I had two sisters, three brothers, and Mom and Dad were dedicated partners to each other and to our family. I had success in school. My dad, who was bigger than life itself, was someone I loved deeply. The security of my young life also extended to my aunts, uncles, and cousins. We all lived, for the most part, on the same street where I grew up.

I was nurtured into my awareness of God and faith through the Catholic faith. I attended church with my family and I graduated from an all girls' Catholic high school. I had every advantage in the world. I had deep faith in the mystical side of life. As a young woman of twenty-two, I was in love, had my future planned with a man whom I felt was my match, and was joyously preparing wedding plans.

And then death entered my life.

My dad, whom I adored and believed would be with me into old age, had been diagnosed with cancer a year and a half earlier. He had survived and fought his way through the disease and I simply did not believe…I simply could not allow myself the truth…that he was a dying man. Within eighteen months of his diagnosis, he was gone. Determined to walk me down the aisle the day of my wedding, he lost that battle, too.

The shock of loss, coupled with my youthful heart, simply could not hit the pause button. I had no tools, no way to grace myself with time and space to heal. My world was spinning out of control. I was numb and I did what I felt I needed to do. I married my fiancé. With dad gone, my marriage assured my place in the world. My brothers walked me down the aisle in Dad's stead. The three of us held each other up on that long church aisle. My family, also numb with grief, held each other up through those dark early moments.

Grief's trauma led me into a life I was not ready to live. Sadly, I found myself separated and divorced within three years. Not just from a man, but from the dreams and ideals I had once believed in as a child.

Fast forward twenty years and I was remarried to a wonderful man who was also my business partner. While driving alone in the Arizona desert on a business trip to the Miraval Resort, I experienced a miracle. In an instant, my life was changed forever. From out of nowhere, my life's purpose began playing out on the long winding black ribbon of highway stretched before me.

It was early morning, just past dawn, and as a morning person I was awake, rested, and alert. I was excited about the upcoming weekend of work. The skies were patched with clouds from a storm that had passed through the area. The air had that wonderful "after rain" smell that is clean and fresh. The temperature was crisp on this cold January morning. Everything was amazingly precise. The desert and foothills were bursting with life from the housecleaning effects left by Mother Nature's rainstorm. Everything was normal by my definition. Life was good. And then, suddenly I received "the message."

I was to help people die. Not just help people die, I was to help the caretakers and families who were tending to the dying.

At the time I received the inspiration, I thought it was a little strange. I understand any skepticism my readers may have as I share this. Whatever others may feel, I felt it times ten at the time! I began asking all kinds of mental questions. They flew around my car, bouncing off the doors, windows and roof like ping pong balls flying around a concrete room. For every thought I hit away, another one appeared.

Why me? How? I must be crazy...am I crazy? Am I hearing things? The message felt so crystal clear. It was not a voice per se, it was more a thought but one I didn't initiate. On this crystal clear, beautiful desert morning, the idea of death was not on my radar. It was not even in my immediate universe.

I had not given much credence to the fact that over a span of eighteen years, I had been blessed to care for my maternal and paternal grandmothers, my mother-in-law, and my Aunt Mary in their final hours before their deaths. As Soul Sitters continues to unfold, it is their wisdom and my personal experiences with them that inspire what I now lovingly refer to as the *Soul Sitter Movement*. I think of them as part of my "upstairs team" and I lovingly refer to them as my Mother Guides.

Even as I acknowledged this fact in my now changed life, I still sometimes felt overwhelmed. This was not a common experience for me. Helping people die was not part of my life plan, at least not as I knew my life plan to be.

I had a career as a photographer. I was in a happy marriage. I was fulfilled. Why would I want to do such a thing? What credentials did I have? I was not qualified for such a task. I took pictures of babies and children and families. I took pictures of business women and helped them brand their careers. I simply did not involve myself with death outside my own family.

Given all my mental arguments, I felt compelled to ask for confirmations. I looked up, taking my eyes away from the road and asked the air to help me know I was not crazy. The "air" complied almost immediately, as a cemetery in the middle of nowhere appeared over the next knoll of the highway

For the next three days, I received one confirmation after another that the message was real and valid.

By Sunday, for various reasons, I was convinced. I was meant to do this work. I had no idea how or what it would look like. I simply knew that I had to do it; that I was willing to do it; that I was committed. As I drove home to San Diego from the Tucson resort of Miraval, I was determined. I stepped out in faith and while my faith has challenged me at many points on this journey, each and every moment has been a rich and fulfilling experience.

The gift I received is intended to be paid forward. That is my work. That is the purpose of Soul Sitters. Perhaps at some level, the purpose of humanity is to soul sit each other through difficult and challenging times.

Once back at home, I began to consider what each of my soul sitting experiences with my four Mother Guides had in common. The following pages reveal a series of tools and exercises that will help you, and hopefully, nurture you (the soul sitter) as you work through your loss, whether you are currently in this situation or whenever you face it in the future.

Keep in mind that loss has many layers. Like anyone, I have experiences that remind me of my dad. It has been twenty years since I lost my dad and I continue to discover new tenderness that belongs to my own loss. Through grace, I have been taught that all the emotions I continue to feel are okay. In fact, they are normal and natural. On one of Oprah's last shows, Toni Morrison (author and Nobel Prize recipient) spoke of her son's death and the ongoing emotions she still felt even years later. She beautifully, and without regret, explained that she continues to grieve his death, that she is still saddened. She went on to say that if he could get sick and die, she could honor his death with her grief. Her peaceful acceptance of her ongoing sadness gave me permission to sometimes feel the sadness of my dad's death, even twenty years later. For me, it erased in a sweet way, any form of guilt I had that insisted I "get over it." Yes, we have to continue living; no, we do not have to fill the aching space with anything. The good news is that through healthy sadness we continue to be connected to our loved ones. Through healthy sadness, we are never alone. We never lose anyone, even as our heart breaks.

So I continue to unpeel my layers of loss. It has taken me years to decipher the meaning within those layers. When I find myself facing a road overgrown with doubt and riddled with potholes of discouragement, I remember my dad's courage as a businessman and father. His living example softens my heart. I am further reminded that he loved his family deeply and never shied away from a challenge. Together with my mom, he taught me the tremendous value that comes from living fully, even though at times I may want to curl up and take a twenty-year nap, reverting to happy memories with my dad.

My hope is that, as you read these chapters, you will find solace and helpful information. You do not have to brave, choke down or stuff your feelings; you do not have to remove yourself emotionally from your experience. You can be with your own sadness and still be present for the person you love, with dignity, grace, and peace. You can add to the value of their life as they transition into death.

As I reflect on my losses, I cannot help but compare my life experiences with what I see happening in the world today. There is so much loss, far more traumatic than my own. Families are asked daily to face the loss of their loved ones due to wars, terrorism, and the hideous nature of cancer and other life-threatening diseases. I think of how people have suffered the more public losses of our time and my prayer is for these 'steps' to be a lifeboat, helping others navigate the stormy sea of life and death. The promise they bring is one of being helpful, healing, and holistic.

When life meets death, there is no way around, only through. I am deeply hopeful these tools will offer you courage, permission to be yourself, and comfort for you and your loved one, as he or she passes.

# Chapter Two
# The Steps

*Absence sharpens love; presence strengthens it.*

Benjamin Franklin

I am reminded of an experience my husband Daniel and I had climbing Diamond Head in Honolulu, Hawaii, years ago. Taking one step at a time, I wondered, "When is this going to end?" The climb was exhausting but when I arrived at the vista, it was soulfully rewarding. Once I reached the top, my muscles stopped firing and I relaxed down to my bone marrow. Before me, was the majesty of the Pacific Ocean and the Hawaiian Islands. I would never have witnessed the islands from this vista had I not been willing to climb the winding path leading to the top.

Hiking to the summit of any experience can leave you with the sense that all your energy has been drained. . It takes great effort to make the climb. But once the top is reached, and taking in a deep breath, the view is transformational. But once we arrive at the top, if we can stop and take a deep breath, the view that greets us is always transformational. My initial reaction to Soul Sitters was the mountain I had just climbed. I was exhilarated but unsure of the view. I was also uncertain how to go forward.

Fortunately, Daniel and I had planned a much needed vacation that became my renewing breath. Three weeks after my visit to Miraval, we found ourselves in the luxury of a parent-free – work-free – vacation in Santa Barbara. It felt like a second honeymoon. It was early February and we were met by eighty degree temperatures and clear skies. We were vacationing with two good friends and had rented bikes. As we headed south, riding along the Santa Barbara boardwalk, we basked in the sun and the view of the Pacific Ocean.

I was so peaceful and relaxed. Adorned in my baseball cap, I was having such a wonderful time and I felt connected to everyone I met. I had fallen back from the group only by a few yards, peddling at my own slower pace. I was simply taking in the natural landscapes and nature reserves, south of the Santa Barbara Zoo. I truly believe this was a lesson unto itself. It was in the womb of nature, free of troubles and completely focused on the moment that I received another message. I was refreshed at the time, making eye contact with passersby and my mind was unworried and unhurried.

The "how to" of Soul Sitters unfurled, like a movie preview. Remember when you were a kid and flipped through a series of drawings formed into a tiny book that animated the figures as you quickly fanned the pages? One, two, three, four, five; they became clear, precise, exact. The acronym "STEPS" just popped into my head as I thought about how many steps there were to this process I had been doing. How much simpler could any direction be? In all my years as an entrepreneur, trying to come up with slogans and ideas that communicated my work, I had never had anything come to me so readily. I was not brainstorming for information. I was not trying to "come up with" something. In my relaxed state, I simply received clarification.

I realized another piece of the "how-to" puzzle of getting the Soul Sitters' message across had fallen into place. Buoyed with confidence, I knew it was simple and something that everyone could easily remember. It was elementary and yet profound at the same time. I knew that having this clear message would make a significant difference in the lives of people everywhere.

Two days later, Daniel and I were peddling to have breakfast. We were following the same path and passed the site where I had received the message. The beauty seemed even more radiant than before and I was so excited to point out "the spot" to Daniel. As we continued our bike ride further down the boardwalk, true to my experience on the way to Miraval, I received another confirmation. Off to my right, overlooking the Pacific Ocean, a cemetery rose up to meet me. Perhaps it seems strange to call the cemetery "a miracle" but that is how it felt. Its unexpected appearance felt like an affirmation from my Mother Guides. It was a replay moment of my trip to Miraval.

The "STEPS" that are revealed in this book are skills you can keep in your back pocket until you need them. Like money in your hand, they have lasting, timeless value and can be employed by anyone. My personal experience has taught me that employing them is healing for both the patient and the soul sitter. To sit with someone who is dying is an opportunity to experience life at its pinnacle. Using the STEPS can be a transformational and life-changing experience, building confidence and ease as the soul sitter guides others to meet death's impact. I understand and I am not insensitive to the complexity of that impact; it takes tremendous courage. But regret is an awful thing to live with, and summoning up the courage to make this very personal connection is powerful, especially if you are uncomfortable with, or afraid of, loss. It is hard for everyone to let go of loved ones. The STEPS are a lifeboat for many and there are simply no words that I can use to explain their priceless value.

As difficult as death is, it may be one of the only times in life that we have an opportunity to be totally present with another human being. The mental, emotional, or spiritual shift that comes through these STEPS is compelling. It is not unlike the breathtaking view I experienced once I reached the top of Diamond Head.

## THE STEPS

We can know in our heads that death is real. At the same time, it feels contradictory to life. It is never easy and is sometimes untimely, and feels unjust. As I look back at my own experiences, I can honestly say the deaths of my loved ones would have been easier had I had some tools. Going through the same STEPS with each of my four Mother Guide's deaths would have offered my heart and lungs space. I don't pretend to believe that the sadness, grief and tears will be removed. What the STEPS offer to your experience with death is acceptance for what it is — and perhaps therein a sense of peace may be felt both mentally and physically.

Regardless of where you find yourself in faith or belief, these STEPS are universal. They are STEPS for soul sitters to be sure, but they go far beyond that. They have the power to transform personal relationships with loved ones, friends, and even casual acquaintances into a work of art. These STEPS are portable, like a step-stool you would use to reach something that was out of reach. They are a way of engaging people and relating to them in a profound and authentic way, placing into your hands tools that work.

It is my honor to share these with you. The acronym "STEPS" stands for:

### Smile

### Touch

### Eye Contact

### Patience

### Service

The STEPS offer a method that brings people together with dignity and respect for all humankind. Offering them to the world seems not only kind, but required.

### SMILE

*Smile though your heart is aching*
*Smile even though it's breaking...*

To smile when encountering death may feel counterintuitive. When we first learn of a loved one's diagnosis or terrible accident, our hearts tend to tighten up and it is natural to hold our breath. Many kinds of emotions surface: Fear, anxiety, the intense feelings of hopelessness and need to fix the situation can be overwhelming. Tears are the natural voice of the heart; they are tender and convey your love. It was very clear to me when given the STEPS that the first step was not meant to mask grief or sadness. Offering your smile to your loved one through your tears is not only acceptable, it is authentic and real.

If you want to open hearts or minds, put a smile on your face. Nothing eases an awkward moment faster than a smile. Even when your heart is aching, breaking, a smile on your face can tell patients that you are present and happy to be to be with them, regardless of the circumstances. By acknowledging how precious each moment is, you reaffirm they are an important part of your life. This can be accomplished regardless of whether you are sitting by their side throughout the day or if you only have occasional in-person visits or telephone conversations with them. Your support and love in any capacity during this time has deep, everlasting value.

The first time anyone does anything, practice is critical to how well we do. Every time death meets life is a first time for the dying person and for that exact experience with you. It is natural to feel lost and anxious before your visits. If you want to make the experience easier and more meaningful for you and your loved one or friend, wisely prepare yourself before you walk into the room. Simply stop and let your tongue release off the roof of your mouth. This will relax your jaw. Take a deep breath and hold to count of five, then slowly breathing out to the count of five. Check to make sure your breath is even, and if you are still tense, repeat the exercise. Bring to mind a happy memory of a time you and the person spent together. Perhaps, even make a list before your visit so you have a tangible reminder. As you walk into the room, allow the corners of your lips to move upward, not in a full smile but relaxed, communicating your caring and gratitude for seeing them. Your smile is medicine for the person, pain free with no side effects.

The greatest need for anyone, regardless of circumstance, is the need to remain valid and valued as a human being. When you offer a smile to someone, you see him; not as a sick person, but as a valid and valuable person who still contributes. His life has meaning. Such a gift cannot be underestimated or undervalued. A smile, when given genuinely, says, "I am so happy to have this moment with you. I care about you, I value you and I validate the person you are." A smile is contagious and can infect, in a positive way, everyone in the room.

## TOUCH

For me, when my family members were dying, they longed to be touched. Admittedly, some people feel uncomfortable being touched. To complicate the issue, there are some professionals who feel this may be overreaching. So keep in mind, unless it is a light touch to their hand or arm, ask the person for permission.

Science has proven, beyond a shadow of doubt, that safe touch is the single most important gift we can offer. On a large scale, touch is a very basic need and wholly underestimated in the role it plays in helping people feel connected and valued. As I received the STEPS, it was clear to me touch was of vital importance.

On a physical level, the human body is an energetically charged, electrical miracle with thirty-seven miles of nerve endings woven throughout. This electrical highway continually sends impulses to our brain. The brain then processes the information in the synaptic flashes and issues orders to our senses. Even though for most this energy seems intangible, it is nonetheless powerful, viable and palatable. To touch someone, even if lightly on the arm, lets them know at a deeply visceral level that you care for them. It is true that your mere presence can effectively change a person's experience; but to touch them is to put a lit match to the candle's wick. They will feel not only where your hand touches their arm, but they will register it in their heart.

I have found through experience that the best and most preferred place to touch someone in pain is to touch them on their hands or forearm. It is a safe place that most people welcome. Others may invite you to massage their head or feet. Some loved ones who are bedridden find great relief when their legs are massaged. A wonderful means for breaking down resistance is to apply lotion to areas of skin that are dry. Any act of touch is a selfless act of loving service. We are reaching out through our humanity and making contact with another human being. Touch is a fundamental need for every living being on the planet

The most beautiful thing about touch is that it follows eye contact. Often, once eye contact is made, barriers are naturally broken down and a connection is made. In some cases, touch may follow the next STEP, eye contact. This is where practical application of the STEPS is important. Remember, the goal is to help the patient feel comfortable and loved, not to follow a rigid recipe. You will know which STEP to take, in what order, if you are paying attention and listening.

## EYE CONTACT

It is said the eyes are the window to the soul. This comes from ancient wisdom and can be found in the New Testament: Matthew 6:22-23 and has been quoted down through the ages, from Dante to Churchill. I offer this information to show you the practical side of its application. Truth be known, Western culture does not necessarily lend itself to this practice. The power of simply looking into someone's eyes is more profound than anything you might have to say to them.

There is spiritual power in eye-consciousness, the ability to connect with someone through the window of their soul. Casual eye contact is understood. We make eye contact every day with the checkout clerk, the barista, our neighbors and community we shop with. But there is a significant difference between casual eye contact and acknowledging their humanity. It is a common interpretation to assume that someone who does not make eye contact is hiding something. When entering the room of a loved one, avoiding eye contact tells that person you are hiding, too. If you have smiled, your body will most likely have relaxed. If you follow the smile with a light touch, you have engaged your loved one and assured him or her of their place in the world. When you look into their eyes, they will feel connected and acknowledged.

Eye contact breaks down barriers and allows your heart to open. By this simple conscious act, you will experience something that may surprise you. You not only see the person differently, but more importantly, you will FEEL the person differently. Eye contact for the soul sitter offers an emotional charge that is full of love, acceptance, and compassion. The benefit of eye contact is reciprocal. You too will feel connected and valued.

In Dr. Jill Bolte-Taylor's personal story of experiencing a stroke, she describes how isolated she felt within her own body. In her book, *Stroke of Insight* she described how she could think inside her mind but could not communicate to the outside world. The only way she could feel trust for anyone was if they made eye contact with her. Whenever they did, in her mind she just kept repeating, *"I am here, come in and get me."* (You can hear her remarkable story by searching www.youtube.com.) She forever changed how I look into another person's eyes. I think we intuitively know the importance of eye contact. At some level, we echo Dr. Bolte-Taylor's mindful call: *I am here, come and get me.* We all long to know we are not invisible.

## PATIENCE

When I received the STEPS in Santa Barbara, it became evident that patience is more than a virtue, it's crucial. We need inner strength to be patient, even when we are unaware of the source of that strength. Humans are, for lack of a better word, a squirming lot; if we are not squirming in body then we are squirmy in mind. The reaction of squirming is simply a manifestation of our discomfort and results in impatience. We want the moment to pass because nobody likes sitting in discomfort. We can only be patient with others after we have learned to become patient with ourselves.

Patience is a state of being, not a destination. We have all felt that rising foam of impatience, cutting us off from the moment we are experiencing. It is only by practicing patience that it can become natural and organic. There is no shortcut to achieving patience. We simply choose it. I wish I could tell you that old anxieties will disappear at once if we do choose it. Unfortunately, that is not true. When we first "try to be patient" the old habits can return with hurricane force. So be kind to yourself if you tend to be an impatient person. Choosing patience can be challenging. As I said earlier, death is always a "first" regardless of how often you are faced with it. Your patience muscle must be built over time.

**Techniques for Building the "Patience Muscle"**

In times of stress, impatience is our default switch. The only viable tool to combat stress is to breathe deeply, in and out, and then repeat this process until you feel a sense of calm returning to your body and mind. Even-paced breathing will slow anxiety-driven impatience down. You will learn to recognize when your anxiety is moving you away from the present moment. You will want to be anywhere but where you are. Breathing deeply can calm the early stages of butterflies and quell a full-blown anxiety attack. Our breath is the most powerful sedative we have. It is on duty, 24/7/365 and always available. We just need to be aware of its power.

To practice breathing, fill your lungs with air, hold it for a moment, and then quietly and quickly exhale it out through your nose or mouth. Often one breath will be enough to calm all the electrical energy sparking through you. Your mind, body, and spirit will respond to this act of inhaling and exhaling and you will find yourself with the fresh frame of mind you need to face the stressful situation with patience. The process only takes a moment or two, so it is worth the effort to take a mindful breath. You will feel rooted and aware.

There are so many avenues that can help build a strong patience muscle. Meditation has gone mainstream and what the ancient masters understood, medical science now acknowledges. Doctors recommend that even fifteen minutes a day of silent meditation can improve your health. It reduces stress, lowers blood pressure, and can even help dissipate hot flashes — just to name a few symptoms. Other methodologies include yoga, Qigong, Tai Chi, walking meditations, or even reading inspirational or spiritual material. You can also include in this list stroking your pet or listening to music; anything that will calm the mind will strengthen the patience muscle. As you increase your patience muscle through breathing, you will experience a greater sense of calm.

The next scenario you may face when soul sitting is silence. It can feel like a fog has settled in over a room and filled up the space between you and your loved one. Our Western culture does not feel comfortable with this kind of silence. Additionally, impatience and anxiety cannot honor silence. The natural first response is to talk. It is my first default in any situation where silence is trying to be heard; I am always inclined to fill it with my voice.

If you feel a need to speak only as a means to fill the silence, press your foot into the floor as if you were putting on the brakes. Let the silence simply be. There is profound communication that stretches through the airwaves in the space of silence. At this point, you have smiled and perhaps you are touching your loved one; you have made eye contact and she knows you can see her. Each one of the STEPS is like an angelic partner, and patience will lead to personal comfort and a more loving heart, even in silence.

## SERVICE

In this process, you have smiled, touched, made eye contact and activated patience, and now you are prepared to serve. A person facing the final frontier of life deserves to be served. What else can the patient receive at this place in life but service? Jewel, the singer/songwriter wrote, "In the end, only kindness matters." Service is the ultimate form of kindness.

Even though there may be nothing you can do, the simple act of intention is valuable and loving. Service can include big things, like caretaking in the last days of a person's life. It can mean providing dinners to the caretakers and their families. Service can include driving people to doctor's appointments or making sure a pet is taken to the vet or being walked and fed. It can also include tedious household tasks that help maintain order and continuity in their lives. Seemingly unimportant acts are just as important to the other person as big tasks. Service is showing up for what is needed and is not akin to either "big" or "small." It is, quite literally, acting from the state of love. As Louisa May Alcott said, "Love is the only thing we can carry with us when we go…"

Service is not limited within the framework of the living. You can continue to be of service after the person has died, too. My experience with this came when my Aunt Mary requested that I burn her journals. A friend's brother-in-law asked her to take his dog. To serve is to surrender yourself and your needs, if only for a short time. It is an emptying of self and subscribed to by every spiritual master who has ever taught humankind. It does not mean martyring yourself; it simply means sharing whatever resources you may have available: your time, your talent, your shoulder. There is no such thing as the "wrong" service. We all have gifts and abilities, and the ordinary things we already know how to do become extraordinary acts of kindness when we do them for others.

~ ~ ~ ~ ~ ~ ~ ~ ~ ~ ~ ~ ~ ~

As a whole, the STEPS are ideal for expressing love and concern to a dying person. You never have to be careful about saying or doing the right thing when you follow the STEPS. Understand that you have the power to make an enormous difference in the last days, hours or minutes of a person's life.

At the same time, I want to emphasize that you do not have to wait until a person is ready to pass from this world before you use these STEPS. It is my hope and prayer that people will begin using the STEPS in everyday life experiences, because it will transform relationships. It will transform you, too. Why wait until the end of life to let friends or family know how much you love them or that they matter to you?

I have had some wonderful moments with people when I have centered myself and communicated with them using the STEPS. Life can be uncomplicated if we only give ourselves permission to see through the confusion to its simplicity and order. I do not mean to minimize the unpleasant or unwanted things that show up; but I do feel there is no challenge or problem that does not come with a solution. The STEPS can be a simple solution — not necessarily easy, but simple. Employing them has the ability to bring healing and joy to souls, both to those who will be sojourning upon the earth for a long time yet to come, and for those who will be departing soon. With the power to transform relationships, STEPS are the guardian angels we can all shake hands with.

## WHEN YOU CANNOT BE THERE

Sometimes life's circumstances limit your interaction with the person who is dying. Geographically, you may be in a position to Soul Sit from a distance. Your support and love is felt, whether or not you are next to a person or reaching out from a distance. We live in the age when communicating across geographic distances is cost effective and can be easy if each party has computer access. Admittedly, this is not the same, but be assured by reaching out, no matter the form, you are making a difference.

The heart and soul value of reaching out via phone, mail or technology (such as Skype) allows us the grace needed at a time like this. If you decide to make a phone call or Skype with loved ones who are still independent and healthy enough to connect in this way, make sure you set aside time to listen to them exclusively. Shut off your iPad, your computer, and put down your "to do" list. Your gift to them is the gift of your time, so make sure to set aside at least a half-hour or more to simply listen.

All the STEPS (and ideas that follow this chapter) apply when you are geographically separated. If you Smile when someone answers the phone, even if you are in tears, the person on the other end of the line will feel your sincerity through the airwaves. If you can be honest and sincere and reach out to others' sadness, fears, or other emotions, they will feel your Touch. If you are paying attention to what they are saying, they will feel seen. By not interrupting, they will feel your Patience. You will know how to serve them, what is needed and what is within your capabilities if you are doing the other four things.

Most importantly, do not feel guilty for being unable to travel to them (or if you are simply choosing to stay so your own family's needs are met). Our life priorities are important and sometimes those priorities take precedence. Be kind to yourself and let your situation simply be what it is — which is okay. The many ideas in *Soul Sitters* offer ways and means to "soul sit" whenever and wherever you are in your life.

## THE STEPS

**S** – Smile

Authentically and with your whole body

**T** – Touch

Administered with permission and respect

**E** – Eye Contact

To acknowledge the dying's humanity

**P** – Patience

Giving space and reverence to their environment

**S** – Service

Your gift in action, not material things

# Chapter Three
# White Space on the Map

*Stand still. The trees ahead and the bush beside you are not lost.*
DAVID WAGONER, "LOST"

I once heard an interview on National Public Radio (NPR) with an author who described the unknown and unexpected part of life brilliantly. He suggested that every person has a life map and the roads we travel, for the most part, are known to us. By his analogy, we rarely venture into unknown territories beyond our own familiar space. But every so often, we find ourselves off the familiar and on "white space," where there is no familiar road to travel on. Unexpected white space can be a disconcerting feeling, one that topples us and leaves us feeling vulnerable and even fearful. Death and dying is for most of us the white space on the map.

The STEPS are easy to understand and offer a wonderfully simple and mapped country road to walk down. They ease the way and give soul sitters actual tools that will help create a space of trust and intimacy with the person dying. They are powerful and if they become the only thing used from *Soul Sitters*, then they would be enough for many. The insights that come when using them have the potential to offer you peace and wisdom that goes far beyond your own reasoning. They are easy to share with others and useful, even in our day-to-day living relationships. But sometimes, a deeper understanding is desired and longed for when it comes to death and dying.

Death is the great mystery; it is the ultimate white space. Perhaps contemplating it would be a distraction as we navigate the familiar roads of our life map. At the same time, death's mystery is something often ignored until we come face-to-face with it. We do that in so many ways, either through joking, ignoring, avoidance, or even absence.

Even though we see death every day, even though we witness it in nature, or with a pet, or a vase of flowers, we simply move past it in a blind acceptance. Given the propensity to avoid the subject, our human nature moves us around it and not through it. We even avoid the word "death," using catch phrases such as "leaving" or "gone." Death is to life what the sand is to the ocean. The first person to break down this barrier was Dr. Elisabeth Kübler-Ross. In her work, she demonstrated how the emotions of death, when misunderstood, can turn into riptides that pull us away from our sense of feeling rooted and stable.

A woman of decidedly unique views from an early age, Kübler-Ross was one of the first mainstream doctors and authors to offer insights on the process people go through when facing their own deaths. As a young woman of sixteen, she volunteered during World War II, helping out in hospitals and with refugees. The turning point in her life came at the end of the war when she visited the Majdanek concentration camp and witnessed the art work that had been left behind by the prisoners that had died there. Carved into the walls of the camp were hundreds of images of butterflies, whispers of hope left behind by the victims of Hitler's insane death sentences. It does not surprise me that I was inspired to choose the butterfly as a symbol for my book.

Elisabeth Kübler-Ross immigrated to the United States from Switzerland in 1958, where she completed her education in the field of psychiatry. Her professional work (and I believe her purpose and heart) continually led her to care for terminally ill patients. The insights she gained from her work were so inspiring and insightful that she documented them in her book *On Death and Dying* (first published in 1969). At the time of its publication, her work revolutionized how professionals and the general public perceived death.

In her work, she encouraged others to talk to those who are dying and listen to them, giving them permission to express their feelings and wishes. She recognized how unresolved issues make the process more painful and encouraged others to help, if at all possible, resolve issues that the dying person may be holding onto. This falls into the Service category. As you come to embrace and understand Kübler-Ross's now commonly recognized "5-Stages of Death and Dying[1]," resolution of unsettled life accounts may be one of your greatest gifts to the person dying. But it can also be tentative for sure, and if you feel ill-equipped for this task, then your service can be to employ a counselor or pastor to speak with the patient.

It is important for me to reassure anyone who is a soul sitter that I recognize this is not a simple or easy process. While the STEPS and Dr. Kübler-Ross's insights into the five stages of death

---

[1]    Kübler-Ross, Elisabeth, *On Death and Dying*, Touchtone, 1969

are remarkably effective, the landscape of what you are facing is unpredictable. Each death will have many shades, tones, and colors, with different textures and patterns. This is the only time in anyone's life experience that is indisputably uncertain, foggy and foreign. It is white space on the map and no one can reassure you of what your own experience will be like. I can only tell you that as a soul sitter, our ability to face the truth of the situation is paramount. The circumstances cannot be fixed, changed or repaired. The feelings can only be felt, not erased. It will be your natural inclination to want to reassure or try to make feelings different or better. It is genuinely uncomfortable to be with those who are dying while they are processing their emotions around their own death. It has been my experience that the STEPS alleviated that to some degree for me. They grounded and stabilized my emotions when those emotions wanted to lead me away from my purpose. Partnering them with other tools only makes them more valuable.

Before I share the 5-Stages with you, I want to encourage you, if you would like more in-depth details, to read Dr. Kübler-Ross's books. She has authored more than twenty publications on the subject of death and dying and a partial list can be found in the glossary. Before I enter into the 5-Stages, please be aware that I have done some of my own interpretive work; the use of italics below is an indication of a direct quote from *On Death and Dying*.

I leave you with Elisabeth's own words:

> *"...although there is no set, proper way to die, the stages of grief are fairly common, and apply not only to the dying patient but the family as well."*

## THE 5-STAGES OF DYING

### DENIAL

Denial is the strongest defense system we have as human beings. It is most often the first of the stages because endings represent just that — endings. We all resist endings and, as a species called "human," we resist and resent change. The state of denial is our 'sergeant of arms,' the guard at the door that keeps change and death at arm's length. If the person dying does not have a spiritual foundation or a feeling of being eternal, then death represents the final chapter. *"Denial acts as a buffer and may be firmly in place, even to the end. The reaction to denial is related to shock and is a way of coping..."*

As a soul sitter, Dr. Kübler-Ross recommends that *"...The... loneliness, fear and denial responses experienced by patients should be handled by others with acceptance and understanding, instead of contradiction."* It is important not to press someone into reality when in this state. The outcome will not change; but if cornered, the process will change dramatically — and it will change for everyone's experience — and not necessarily for the better.

### ANGER

Not being heard is one of the single worst experiences of life. We think we hear, but truth be told, we do not listen. Sometimes, it is because we do not know what we do not know and have no tools to respond. Other times, we hear "interpretively" and make assumptions that are incorrect. Then there are the times when we feel awkward and listen long enough to respond politely before we take a fast exit out of the room. To be faced with our own death and to have no one who is willing to hear us is the greatest emptiness of all. Not only have those with fatal diagnoses lost control over their lives, but they have disappeared in many respects. The level of frustration a dying person (or even their loved one) would experience is volcanic in nature, creating either a weeping or raging volcano of anger.

Kübler-Ross explains: *"Ordinary life continues and the patient feels he is already being considered deceased by the rest of the world."* I do not believe it is intentional on anyone's part; it is simply part of the process. Soul sitters and/or the family of the soon to be deceased feel this sting, especially in a hospital setting when the dying patient is in pain or has any kind of need that seems to go unmet. There is a lack of sense of urgency that comes with being ill until code blue is sounded. Not being heard, having our needs go unmet, all sum up to feelings of being invisible.

As expressed in the STEPS, I want to emphasize that to be seen, acknowledged, and heard is not only important as a human being; it is the single most important and shared need by everyone on the planet.

My only personal experience with anger came when I suggested to Dad that my wedding could be scaled down with the ceremony being performed in our family living room, with him in his favorite chair. I even went so far as to suggest he could be in his pajamas. His reply was emotionally charged, although not explosive. He only mildly displayed his temper, emphasizing that he would be the one to walk me down the aisle. In my youthful innocence, I simply accepted his strong position without question and was unknowingly able to give him the satisfaction of still being my dad. He was not invisible.

The best antidote is to listen. *"...take the time to understand that the deprivation of communication, fear, and frustration contributes to the anger. If the companion or the family is not afraid of death, and not defensive, we can listen to the anger and understand expressing it is a relief to the patient."* It is so very difficult to be objective and not take another's anger personally. The most important thing to remember is that this is VERY personal...to the person who is dying. We may be in pain and be participating in the experience, but <u>we are not having the experience</u>. Soul sitters have the luxury of tomorrow and when tomorrow comes, we can grieve. In the meantime, we just need to listen and not contradict.

## BARGAINING

We begin our life as a child bargaining with our parents, hoping to exchange something we don't want for something we do. It may be to avoid bedtime for another story or avoid eating our peas if we eat more mashed potatoes instead. It is a natural response to barter against something we do not want to happen. Bargaining is an *attempt to postpone the inevitable*. When people are faced with the end of their lives, the same response <u>is</u> inevitable. Dr. Kübler-Ross offers the following example: *Many terminal patients promise to dedicate their lives to God in exchange for additional time to live.*

If we have lived long enough, it is quite certain that we understand that bargaining is not always effective, especially given a diagnosis of a terminal disease. When my dad was ill and dying in the hospital, I wanted him to be the one to walk me down the aisle. I can honestly say that I don't remember if I did bargain with God at the time, but I wanted to. I wanted the end delayed or avoided altogether. As his daughter, I tasted this bitter fruit. It has helped me empathize with the dying.

Bargaining is a natural process and is a very private process. Dr. Kübler-Ross suggests this stage could be tied to unresolved guilt. If this is so, she suggests for us as soul sitters to listen carefully, without commentary. This will create a safe environment for the person "confessing" their guilt, or their fears, or their regrets. If we can help the person by simply offering a shoulder or "soft place to land," then we can help the person make peace with any unresolved issues.

## DEPRESSION

Facing one's death brings into focus, for that person, the personal meaning of his life. In this stage, depression, as it relates to facing one's own death, is brought on by the *realization of loss.* Loss has a different meaning for each person. Perhaps there is sadness for lost opportunities, lost time, or personal regret for how one has chosen to live one's own life. Behind the emotional darkness of depression lies the patients' realization that the life they lived will soon be over and they are powerless to change their circumstances. Any unresolved issues simply add to the weight of depression. *It usually replaces any denial or stoicism for the terminally ill patient.*

Guilt and shame seem to feed the two different kinds of depression that surface for the person dying. One type of depression, Dr. Kübler-Ross describes as "reactive" and the other is "preparatory." The first is by itself, understood; the second form is *part of the process of preparing for separation from the body.*

If the patient is in the preparatory stage of depression, trying to cheer them up by reassuring them that the family will be fine once they have passed is ill-advised and has proven to be ineffective. *It is important to let them express their sorrow at the total loss they are about to endure.* Dr. Kübler-Ross also advises that: *Having the __logistical__ details resolved regarding the family's well-being and placement of the patient can relieve depression.* This is different from trying to cheer them up.

Depression is also a signal that the person dying (or their loved one who may be in depression) is close to coming to terms with the truth. It means the patient is typically in the fourth phase with only acceptance remaining. While feelings of depression are hard to be present with, without the need to fix them, the truth is that the only way to get to the final stage of peace and acceptance is to feel them. Don't try to rationalize someone's feelings away. It is uncomfortable but soothing to the one dying if you can just be present, both ears turned on and tuned in, knowing this stage is normal. Painful as it is, it is needed and you are being of Service by allowing the person to work through this.

## ACCEPTANCE

This stage is often the last stage but any of the 5-Stages can overlap, being experienced in unison or flooding together, much like a wave comes into the shore. Once acceptance is embraced, the patient *now wants to quietly retreat to his [or her] fate, much like a child returning to the womb.* It is not uncommon for this stage to never be realized by the terminally ill patient. That can happen for many reasons; perhaps the state of denial is so embedded in their emotions they never escape. But, in the event of an abrupt or sudden death, there may be little time or opportunity to reach acceptance.

This stage can be especially difficult for the surviving loved ones who can, out of fear of loss, fight for more surgeries or treatments, or just simply find the loss so unbearable that acceptance is not a viable choice. I experienced this with Aunt Mary when she reached this stage and wanted to bring in Hospice. Her husband Bob was not prepared to say goodbye. She had fought such a valiant fight with cancer for seventeen years and had always come back. The subject of getting help with the final stages of her life had to be approached via a casual conversation over dinner.

Again, not everyone is equipped to intervene or traverse such fragile ice. The value is one of awareness. With awareness, we can be more adept at Soul Sitting. It is okay, in fact it is encouraged, that soul sitters have the freedom to seek guidance, assistance, and/or help — not just for the person dying, but for themselves as well. Aristotle's words of advice are well heeded: *"the ultimate value of life depends upon awareness and the power of contemplation rather than upon mere survival. None of us survive life, but the imprint we leave is eternal."*

### David Kessler and Kübler-Ross

Later in Kübler-Ross's life, she encountered a series of debilitating strokes. It was during this time that she became associated with David Kessler, himself a thanatologist, a person who studies death and grief. For ten years, he worked closely with Kübler-Ross and helped her in her personal grieving process as she approached the end of her own life. I truly understand the many layers of emotions that bubble and churn when faced with endings as final as death appears. Even given individual belief systems that are firmly set in place through our religious or spiritual orientations, death is emotional and touches us in very personal ways. In the last nine years of Kübler-Ross's life, she admits she felt the sting of loss in a very personal way.

David Kessler eased that sting. Together, they wrote *On Grief and Grieving*, a beautiful book that expands the purposeful 5-Stages as first put forth by Kübler-Ross herself. His work is insightful and will further help you process your grief, or offer support to those grieving, or both. You can explore his work at www.grief.com as well as read any of his published books (a partial list is located in the index at the back of Soul Sitters).

I believe that it is appropriate to offer you grace at this point in time, with regard to whatever you are going through that lead you to read this book. Death and the responses we all have to the experience are deeply personal and can feel like our life and our world is being ripped apart, even though intellectually, we know that life will seam itself together and continue once the sun comes up. This is especially acute when life ends abruptly. One of Kübler-Ross's final gifts was admission that even having studied it all of her adult life, in the end, grief needed to be felt and expressed. Her personal story is touching, and in her case, the grief she eventually felt was magnified by the grief of her own earlier life experiences. I feel it is fitting to close this chapter with two thoughts — one my own and one of hers.

**My thought:** Give yourself grace in this process, and to the degree possible, give grace to the people whom you soul sit. Allowing freedom of your own grief's expression (or making space and allowance for another) is vital to the healing process.

Whether it be softly crying, sobbing, or even wailing (literally or figuratively), hold yourself and others with compassionate understanding and patience, the tools offered in The Steps.

More importantly, consider Elisabeth Kübler-Ross's final written words on the subject that she knew so well:

*"It is not just about knowing the stages.*
*It is not just about the life lost but also the life lived."*

# Chapter Four
# Positive Grief Method

*When you are sorrowful, look again in your heart, and you*
*shall see that in truth you are weeping for that*
*which has been your delight.*

KAHLIL GIBRAN

Grief comes.

- Its depth can surprise you and its timing seems random.
- It appears as your heart begins to comprehend what your mind knows.
- It can appear when you discover the news that your loved one's life is soon to end.
- Or it may wait until after the person has passed.

The important thing is that you give yourself permission to feel what you feel. This is such an important piece because eventually, your sorrow will come.

There are moments when your stoicism is needed, and so to hold our sadness hostage is required. But in time, our grief must be felt if we are to live and contribute to the good of our own life and the lives of those around us. For most of us, the sorrow of loss is just more white space on your map. When you feel the oceanic tide of sorrow and grief rush over you, this is the time when you become your own soul sitter. Hearing the term "positive grief method" (described throughout this chapter as PGM) may at first feel counterintuitive. To lose someone to death is a heart-wrenching experience. To even apply the word "positive" to it may feel challenging. The person we love cannot be seen, nor can we hear their voice unless it has been recorded somewhere and we certainly are no longer able to pick up the telephone and call them. PGM is not a quick fix to the sadness or grief you may be feeling. It is not a patch kit to be used on those we love who are grieving. It requires us to flex our "Patience Muscle" in a different kind of way.

As the Soul Sitter movement has unfolded, I have met many people who are unable to let go of their sorrow. Others, when faced with the death of a loved one, spent months and even years in depression. I cannot guarantee that using the positive grief method will suspend any of these symptoms. What I do know about putting it into use is that it has the power to take dying patients out of a void and anchor them in hope and possibility. And while hope is not a "tangible thing," it certainly is a very "tangible feeling" that can be like a flashlight for possibility, leading a person from darkness and isolation into sunlight.

I want to reassure you that the positive grief method...

*     Is not a denial of the death experience
*     Is not a denial of your grief or your right to grieve
*     Is not a suggestion that there is any easy "fix"

But it can be...

*     An anchor to validate the emptiness left by death
*     A cushion to rock your aching heart to sleep at night

\*      Reassurance that life continues if allowed to endure
        within your heart

\*      A symbol of the person you loved and lost

\*      A way to find a slice of joy in an otherwise difficult
        relationship

By incorporating PGM into your life, you will find ways to be with your loved ones in memory that are safe and reassuring. By creating a symbol that reminds you of them, you can make a conscious commitment to connect to them. Your faith in life will become stronger when you feel their presence in your heart, in your mind, and in your own life.

Deepak Chopra said it well:

*"...wherever you place your faith, death remains mysterious. No one fully accepts the reassurances being offered by reason or religion. Dying is a natural process, but our attitudes toward it can be very unnatural. Of course, you can be just as afraid of dying before it happens – the fear itself is what needs to be healed."*

*"In every wisdom tradition there is a teaching called "dying unto death," as the New Testament calls it. This means experiencing the truth about dying while you are still alive."*

## CREATING THE SYMBOL

PGM teaches you how to select a symbol that is meaningful and connects you to the person who is passing or has recently passed. This symbol is something that comes to you as a perception or inspiration. It is the kind of thing you will find when you look for it and a gift that will surprise you. It gives you back the art of discovery that was natural as a child. It helps you become very present with your environment and with yourself, so healing can take place. Being lost in the space of grief, one cannot be aware of what is obvious. Science shows us how we feel about something makes a difference with our experience. I am convinced, now more than ever, that our loved ones are never away. We are just fooled because they are not here in person. But often, if not daily, they leave us little signs trying to get our attention. So, I discovered, through my own pain, a way to find solace for my heart and yet stay connected to my loved ones.

Soul sitting yourself at any point in the death process is critical and is the least selfish thing you can do.

## ACCESSING YOUR PGM STRATEGY: SIMPLE EMOTIONAL COMFORT

PGM is based upon four pillars that symbolically stabilize grief. By strengthening and giving attention to these pillars, the grief a person feels then becomes healing instead of debilitating. Keep in mind, none of us can do this for someone else, and until the grieving person is ready to reconsider a change of perspective, any peace of mind may be difficult to achieve. Some things simply take time. But you can be an example and a torch bearer and lead the way for others.

PGM, like methodologies used in *The Steps and Triads*, is action oriented. To ready yourself, there are actually conscious exercises you can do that will assist you. As a soul sitter, this method is easily taught and shared with others. It can even be mimicked by you and mirrored for another whose aching heart and blurred teary eyes are unseeing.

**Practice the Pillars of PGM**

Awareness and presence is essential to this process and it begins with breath. Turn your attention to your breath, preferably by choice, but even if you are having a deeply emotional moment, when your heart is hurting and the world has stopped turning for you, focusing on your breath is the first step. It is the first thing we subconsciously change when we are feeling tension. It becomes shallow and held and our shoulders tighten and lift toward our ears. It is simply the way of humankind, to hold our breath when we are upset or under stress. Your breath is the first PGM strategy because it is so critical for you to refocus your emotions. By simply acknowledging what you are feeling and then taking a simple action, you can reset your mental and emotional response to anything.

You do this by simply shifting your attention to your heart, to the area in the center of your chest, then place your hand there. Now notice the rise and fall of your chest, while you let your thoughts go by and keep your attention on your heart, breathing in and out.  You can let yourself imagine the heart muscle as a balloon, gently filling up on the inhale, and slightly deflating on the exhale. When you allow yourself to smile gently upon your heart during the breaths, you will be able to increase your heart-brain connection to reset your emotions. We often think of the brain as the emotional regulator; however, through research conducted by the HeartMath Institute, researchers have discovered it is actually the heart which sends the message to the brain to balance our emotional responses.

Heart-focused breathing will <u>not</u> stop you from feeling what you are feeling, but will instead give you space and permission to feel it and more easily move through the feelings. So often, emotional energy becomes trapped in our body by our held breath; and in time, the lack of oxygen can create health challenges, both physical and mental. The stress of grief can throw our heart-rate patterns out of balance, making it more difficult in these times of loss. Heart-focused breathing has been shown to synchronize the heart-brain connection, generating a smooth and even heart-rate pattern called heart-rate coherence. This methodology is used by Sara Gilman, MFT, a psychotherapist for over twenty-five years and a Fellow of the American Academy of Experts in Traumatic Stress, with a Master of Science degree in Clinical Psychology. Sara is featured on the Soul Sitter website and offers her insights and answers questions in her monthly column "Ask Sara." She says, "While grief is a natural process, it is important to learn how to activate our built-in resources to help us move through the pain and transitions in life."

- 1st PILLAR:   Breathe into your heart and smile softly

When you are feeling stress, once you have established your equilibrium, just feel yourself smile. Mother Theresa said, *"A smile is the beginning of peace."* As you breathe and smile, you will begin to feel your body relax and you will become aware of the room you are standing in. There is a good possibility that your emotions have been triggered by some sound, smell, or other sensory stimuli. For a friend, it was a song that was being played over the loud speakers in a store. For me, it was the desert that attuned me to my feelings of loss for Aunt Mary. Others I know have been triggered by smells, such as the fragrance of baked goods that remind them of their mother. The reason this is important to acknowledge is simply that it makes you aware and brings you into the present moment.

- 1ST PILLAR: Breathe into your heart
- 2ND PILLAR: Pay attention to where you are

Now that you have done this, give your memory free reign. While breathing, with a slight tender smile on your face, allow the memories you shared with that person to surface. If your eyes are closed, let your imagination roam. If they are open, look around. I mean really become aware of your surroundings, and let the memory speak to you. I truly believe that the person may be near, offering you a chance to capture that memory symbolically. This symbol could be one of a thousand things, which I will explore in a moment.

- 1ST PILLAR: Breathe into your heart
- 2ND PILLAR: Pay attention to where you are
- 3RD PILLAR: Remember

Now, you have given your memory free reign, take a mental picture. We long to remember what was good in the shared life we had or may still have with our loved one. You have taken a breath, you have smiled, and now you are present and paying attention to where you are. We fear we will lose that memory, that tactile sense that the person had been part of our lives. But when you allow a tender memory to float to the surface, you keep the memory of that person alive.

This is especially important for children. In the movie Sleepless in Seattle, the little boy Jonah (played by Ross Malinger) is awakened in the middle of the night with a nightmare. His dad (a widower played by Tom Hanks) goes to him to try and comfort him. Jonah confesses that his memories of his mother are fading and that he cannot remember her or the things that made her special. His dad then tells him the story of how, when she peeled an apple, the skin would stay together in one long spiraling piece. This is a perfect example of finding that tangible "thing" that anchors us to the memories we cherish.

- 1ST PILLAR:   Breathe into your heart
- 2ND PILLAR: Pay attention to where you are
- 3RD PILLAR: Remember
- 4th PILLAR:   Capture

Now that you have built the pillars for PGM, you will be able to give yourself an anchor, a talisman, a tangible memory symbol that you can turn to whenever you feel the space between you and the person you have lost is widening. This symbol becomes the bridge that will keep you connected, not just in heart, but in memory as well. Having the special talisman that pops up now and again tells us that our loved one is not far from us. For the character Jonah, an apple will always remind him of his mother. Giving ourselves such a tender gift heals the heart and soothes our aching souls.

## THE SYMBOL

Symbols tell a story and to have one that reminds you of a life lived with a loved one is powerfully calming and reassuring. Symbols come in as many different sizes and shapes as there are people. Sometimes symbols choose us, other times, symbols are selected. The secret to finding your symbol is your willingness to be calm so you can consciously acknowledge it. The most important thing about your symbol is that it must have meaning for you. What will work for you may not work for other family members or friends because our experiences with our loved one are unique. However, that does not limit them from becoming a family or tribe symbol that many or all family members can relate to.

### Choosing Your Unique Symbol

Once you have used the PGM to calm your emotions, either search the memory that comes to mind or the room you are standing in. If the symbol is to be chosen, it will become evident to you. For me, cowboy boots remind me of my dad. He always wore them and there were many nights in my childhood when there was a competition among my siblings and me as we vied for the right to help him take them off. He would settle back in his recliner with a drink that we had delivered to him and one of us would straddle his leg and begin to pull. He would put his free foot on our behind and push and in the process of getting them off we would fall forward and laugh. It was a moment, the kind of moment that we all remember as his children. His boots were such a tangible symbol for me that I can still hear them clicking across tile. The smell of leather also activates my memories of my dad.

I literally have a mental shelf for my symbols. Any tube of red lipstick triggers a memory of Grandma Green. A tiara reminds me of Grandy. Aunt Mary's collection of angels became my symbol for her. Any chosen symbol for a loved one is something that reminds you of that unique individual. It is a tangible and often a tactile object that links you to your loved one in a positive and loving way.

## The Symbol that Chooses You

My mother-in-law Edna thought of herself as a little bird. At the time she passed away, she was very frail. Doves planted nests outside her window while she was being cared for in our home and never returned after her death. Soon after her death, I was sitting in our backyard, dangling my feet in our hot tub. It was a beautiful day and I was staring off at the horizon when a hummingbird hovered in front of my face.

At the time, I was not looking for a symbol for her. I simply loved her and admired her. She was a dear and kind woman and I was so honored to be with her as she transitioned from this life into her next life. The hummingbird floating in front of me that day left such an indelible print on my heart that I will forever link hummingbirds to my dear mother-in-law. Even though a hummingbird flutters its wings so quickly one is not able to see them, its message for me is the opposite. The day it hovered in front of my face, I had decided that I needed to take a much needed break from my work. Now when I see a hummingbird, I am reminded to slow down. I feel Edna's presence and I slow down. Symbols can have whatever meaning you attach to them.

## The Less Tangible Symbol

Sometimes the symbol that represents your loved one is less specific, less tactile. One person I spoke to told me that the symbol for her mother is a heart. Hearts show up all the time, not just for her, but for her family, when her mother's presence wants to be known. Hearts have appeared inside watermelon rinds, in mud puddles, and mountainsides and even in waves crashing in the surf. The symbol for her father became the stars on a clear moonless night. For someone else, it could be an eagle flying overhead, a fragrance, or even a rainbow.

**Emotional Resolution**

Each person in our life marks us in ways that are often personal, some having greater impact than others. That impact can come at us, to us, and through us in ways that are not easy and sometimes even scarring. Many, if not everyone I know, has lost a relative, loved one, or friend whose way of living felt like "sandpaper to the soul" to everyone around them. For those who have had this experience, there may be one of two responses to their death: relief or apathy. Those mixed emotions can create or bring up feelings of guilt, even when the relief or apathy is justified.

For our family, Grandma Green (while loved and respected) was difficult at times to be around when she was living. For her, life was "black or white," leaving no room for gray and very little wiggle room or compromise for opinions other than her own. Her words were often as shocking as her blood-red lipstick. Critical, and highly prejudiced, her death was grieved, but the high standards she demanded from everyone vanished upon her death. I think we were all a little relieved not to be under her microscope. I can only speak for myself, but I believe most of us felt a little (if not a lot) guilty for feeling relieved. First, I want to reassure you that your feelings under these circumstances are normal and very human. No one feels comfortable under the tyranny of unreasonableness.

If the "someone" in your life who is dying (or who has died) falls into this category, then you may feel lost in your attempt to come to terms with how you feel about that person's death. The Positive Grief Method of using symbols is a beautiful way of reminding us of what is important. The symbol may validate your personal experience with your loved one by reminding you of what NOT to do. My personal Positive Grief symbol for Grandma Green is a tube of red lipstick. For much of the heartache she caused with her judgments and prejudice, I have found a way to skillfully honor her memory. The red tube of lipstick is a reminder to speak kindly to everyone and to remove prejudice or judgment from my perspective or life. This physical reminder is just one of the simple ways to replace a personal angst with a simple token of love.

A life is a terrible thing to waste and the more you can separate the wheat from the chaff of a life, the more emotional resolution you will be graced with. We have come here to be together and learn from one another. If I can learn what NOT to do, if I can learn what DOESN'T work, then my life choices will be made with greater thoughtfulness. If I can make my choices with greater thoughtfulness, then I may be more present to others and especially to myself as I weave my way through difficult and joyful times. If I can be a better version of myself as a result of knowing them, then the challenging persons who have left the planet have served a higher purpose...even if that was not their intention.

**What Happens Next?**

Once you have identified your symbol, there are many different ways to utilize it as your bridge to the person who has died. One way is to create a tactile object that represents the symbol. A silver pin shaped like a musical note could be symbolic of a particular song, or a ceramic planter for herbs or flowers in the shape of a pair of cowboy boots can be symbolic.

Once your symbol has been selected, you will begin to see it when you most need it. It's an amazing thing, and the only reassurance I can offer is this: buy a red car or want one, and you will see red cars everywhere. Life responds to those who are willing to see. It becomes a synchronistic event between you and the person you have lost. My experiences have taught me that the people I love are never far away from me. It is I who wanders off, separating myself from them.

The Positive Grief method will give you a safe place for your grief. The grieving process is ultimately a gift that gives a life taken away back to us, only in a different form. The Positive Grief Method opens our hearts, if we are willing, and the healing begins when our grief is embraced and given support for its expression.

I invite you to share your symbol with others on my website at www.soulsitters.com. If you would like to borrow one from this chapter, please do so. Sometimes we need a little help as we pan for the gold left behind in the waters of life that have just flowed by.

## POSITIVE GRIEF METHOD
## (PGM)

- 1ST PILLAR: Breathe into your heart
- 2ND PILLAR: Pay attention to where you are
- 3RD PILLAR: Remember with your heart
- 4TH PILLAR: Capture a symbol

# Chapter Five
# The Soul Sitter's Stool

*The three legged stool of understanding is held up by history,
languages, and mathematics. Equipped with these three you
can learn anything you want to learn.*

Robert A. Heinlein

We are all learning to reframe our experience with death. Soul
Sitters is equivalent to the formula described by Mr. Heinlein as
quoted above. The methods contained in this book are a welcome
respite for the body and soul, offering a firm stool to confidently
rest upon. Taking into consideration Mr. Heinlein's theory, Soul
Sitters offers a triad for others to consider as they walk through
the necessary tasks when death meets life. Intuitive care is the
language of Soul Sitter, history is the heritage we share with our
loved ones, and advocacy becomes the mathematics. Together,
they all add up to a plan that makes sense for traversing the many
challenges before you. I liken the triad to a three-legged stool.

The triad models below offer actions anyone can take that are
practical and effective. As I considered the role of soul sitting, it
became clear to me that there was more information available
for others when it came to care taking our loved ones. As a tour
guide to my fellow soul sitters, it was my deepest desire to provide

a solid foundation that will make your job and experience as fulfilling as possible. Given the importance of the trine in theology, I find it ironic that the best way to describe these ideas conceptually is with a triad that is represented as a three-legged stool with three rungs. It is upon the solid foundation of this seat that all soul sitters can sit.

## A TRIAD FOR INTUITIVE CARE

- **Empty Self**
- **Avoid Clichés**
- **Utilize "The Steps"**

**Learn to empty the self.** This is an ancient practice that makes room for more. I like to think of this act—and it is an action—as emptying my glass of muddy water so I can replace its contents with fresh, spring water. It is a spiritual practice to be sure, but you do not have to be a Buddhist monk to practice it. Most religious traditions recommend it as a path to peace of mind. To make space within our psyche and perceptions is a sacred and treasured way of stepping aside and allowing the flow of life to move through us. In the end, we are only vehicles that serve a purpose, whether that service is one of mother, father, friend, partner, employee or soul sitter. If we can empty the idea that we might somehow be special or unique in our service and embrace the concept that any action we take is but a gift, everyone benefits to the fullest extent possible. A gift is never held onto by the small self, it is passed onto another by the authentic self, the soul. To be a soul sitter simply means to be present and loving and put all your own needs aside. The wonderful reward is that you will swim in the sacred pool of life that is transformative and priceless.

**Words Carry Energy.** Be consciously aware of the words you use, especially during times of great stress. Have a friend or counselor you can turn to at times when you feel exasperated and frightened. Soul sitters are caring and loving by nature. The hardest thing we ever do as a soul sitter is to watch someone suffer, whether it is physically, mentally, or emotionally. The first automatic response to any of these painful emotions is to try and fix them. So, it is natural and instinctual to turn to clichés that, when spoken aloud, we think will be magic elixirs. There is no such thing. Of utmost importance is the need for soul sitters to recognize the situation **cannot be fixed**. Surrender of our own need for "magic" is not only needed but is an important step in accepting the reality of the situation. When our discomfort leads us to say, "Things will be okay" or "You'll feel better if we watch a funny movie," we unintentionally move away from the very service we are providing.

It is important, if not critical, that we become conscious of our own anxious emotions so we realize the effect they have on our communications with others. If you can, try to stop yourself, listen to the concerns of the person being cared for, and ask yourself "Is what I am about to say true?" You will find, and shockingly so, that your potential comment is not only NOT true, it may sound insensitive to the person you are caring for. More importantly, you may miss the opportunity to have a deeply meaningful connection with that person before he dies.

**Utilize the Five STEPS.** The STEPS that were the seed to my Soul Sitter idea were inspired and came from a truly Divine place. I feel I was entrusted to carry this methodology to others in a safe and caring way. To this day, I am honored and humbled that something greater than myself handed me this task. Not only did the STEPS provide me a tool to create emotional space for the dying, the happy by- product is that I have found them to be effective in all relationships of my life. It provides the kind of intimacy we all long for.

As I mentioned earlier in the book, the STEPS are simple but not always easy. It is challenging to create new mental pathways that redirect our conditioned life responses. The acronym, however, allows you to remember what these STEPS are. In the middle of an emotional crisis. The STEPS can redirect you if you become invested in the power they bestow on you. In some ways, we are all soul sitters to each other. To incorporate the STEPS until they become our automatic response will move us closer to living a fulfilled and connected life. The following information will be invaluable in supporting you in your goal to finding balance (and hopefully a peaceful presence) for you and your loved one.

## A TRIAD FOR ADVOCACY

- **Advocacy**
- **Palliative & Hospice Care**
- **Kübler Ross' 5-Stages**

An advocate is someone who speaks up when someone is unable to speak for themselves. Sometimes, in the course of soul sitting, you may be asked to be the spokesperson or the objective person who advocates for the patient or a loved one of the patient. You may be tending to someone injured, an elder, or maybe even a family member in pain. If the one you are soul sitting for is at death's door, that person could be at any stage: the beginning, the end, or middle of diagnosis or treatment. It may be obvious to you, but different advocacy may be asked of you depending on the stage. The important thing to take into consideration is that you may probably be the only objective voice in the room. You can see how critically important it is for you to be calm, objective, and rational so your advocacy can be effective. You must learn to be the calm in the center of the hurricane.

To be an advocate as a soul sitter asks us to be sensitive without any displays of pity, even when our own hearts are breaking for the family or the patient. A patient advocate makes sure they have the knowledge and information needed to help advocate so that the patient understands the problem and the prognosis. Have the presence of mind to gather the tools and resources necessary to ensure the patient or loved one receives the care needed. Clarify any confusion with medical professionals who understand the patient's medical condition.

Quite often, patient advocacy requires a special knowledge of medicine and the healthcare system. Not all soul sitters will be trained in this manner. It is important not to assume anything as a soul sitter and if you find yourself in this position, simply be the watchperson in the lighthouse. If need be, seek out the professional assistance required when you are faced with various medical or end-of-life issues you do not understand. You do not have to be all things and know everything. You are, quite simply, like a mid-wife to this process. In the same way a mid-wife is not a pediatrician or surgeon, you can take a breath and not take on such heavy responsibilities. Many hospital facilities have a resident patient advocate you can call upon if needed. Your noticing when it is needed is your role in advocating for the patient.

If you are faced with a loved one or friend who has been diagnosed with a terminal illness, let your love lead the way. That person will have some important and personally challenging decisions to make. Perhaps your role as a soul sitter can be one of team captain if the patient turns to you for support or advice. If you believe you are not up for this task, help them seek out someone who can be. That way, your strengths can come into play and your service will be far more effective.

**Educate yourself in palliative and hospice care.** Patients faced with a serious and/or life-threatening diseases receive two kinds of treatment in the United States today. One kind of treatment brings the promise of a cure and the other, palliative care, is focused on alleviating pain during an end-stage illness. Palliative care can be used while curative treatment is occurring, e.g., receiving pain relief while undergoing chemotherapy. Generally, however, palliative care is a means of giving physical comfort to dying people.

Soul sitters will find, at some point, they may be asked to be advocates for palliative care. It is natural to want to preserve the life of the patient, especially if it is someone we are close to and love. But there comes a time for all of us when it IS time to let go. It is important to recognize when that time comes.

As a soul sitter, it can be challenging to be objective but objectivity is critical once the patient reaches the final stages of life. Palliative care often utilizes narcotics to ease the dying person into their final moments. Often, patients at this stage experience high levels of anxiety and administering narcotics will ease the fear, pain, and discomfort of their final hours. This is a very humane and loving act.

If your patient is a Hospice recipient, you will more than likely have been versed on how to do this and provided with the necessary drugs that will help ease their discomfort. Often, morphine is the most common and effective pain medication provided. It will remove the discomfort and is necessary and humane for most patients as they cross into death.

Let's face it, the use of narcotics is a touchy topic. You may be faced with family members who are tentative about using narcotics at this time. But the bottom line is, death is not pretty and there is no good reason to let our loved one suffer. In all honesty, the administering of narcotics often hastens the death of the loved one. None of us wants to expedite the process. We have to, at this stage of our own life however, surrender what we want to the greater good: giving our loved one a peaceful end-of-life experience. For this reason, your personal education on this issue, especially the relevancy and importance of easing the dying person's discomfort, is crucial as an advocate. Acceptance for what is happening will help ground your determination and objectivity. You may find yourself in the position of educator as you not only ease the dying person's transition, but also ease the pain of the loved ones who are saying goodbye.

**Be an advocate of Hospice care.** If you are unfamiliar with Hospice, I encourage you to take time to learn about this amazing and vital organization. There is, for some, confusion regarding the role they play in the ending days of a patient's life. Hospice is sometimes viewed as a place, other times viewed in terms of service. It can be both. Essentially, Hospice care is the provision of medical, psychological and spiritual support given to a dying person and their family members.

It is made up of many health professionals – doctors, nurses, certified nurse's assistants (CNA), social workers, other health professionals and chaplains, as well as volunteers, family and friends. Hospice patients can either be  at death's threshold or have been diagnosed with a terminal illness where the patient may even live for years. One Hospice agent told me they once had a patient for three years, which is very uncommon. They work through religious communities, hospitals, and nursing/elder care homes, ensuring the dignity and respect that the end of life is so deserving.

Hospice can attend to the dying patient in any one of these physical locations: a retirement home, a skilled nursing facility, a hospital, a Hospice Center dedicated to the care of the dying, or in the residence of the patient. My experience with Hospice came as I attended to the needs of my beloved female relatives as they passed away in the comfort of their own homes. I was one of many of their soul sitters and with the assistance of other family members (and Hospice) I witnessed firsthand how important the love and support of Hospice members were, not only for the dying, but for all of us.

Unless soul sitting becomes your vocation or avocation, the opportunity to care for others in this way comes but only a few times in life. Because of the intermittent nature of soul sitting, it is impossible as an individual to be privy to all the care available for the dying. The practical list is endless, including but not limited to medications, narcotics, equipment, and/or procedural protocols. Hospice workers are professionally trained and have access to these resources. Partnering with them takes this responsibility off your and the family's shoulders and allows you to be fully present with the dying person. It also gives you breathing space to take care of the necessary but mundane parts of life: bills, work, carpooling, et cetera.

Upon the death of your loved one, it is necessary to attend to practical tasks. One of the most valuable pieces that Hospice service provides is to guide family members through the required paperwork once the person has died. The Hospice agents understand the emotional tightrope the family is walking and do everything they can to pave a smooth path. We may not expect or want the sun to rise the next day, but it will. Hospice workers understand that life continues after death and that the new day arrives with or without our permission. With it comes the mundane. They also make sure all narcotics are disposed of properly and that all medications are removed from the premises.

I am a supporter of Hospice and I am hopeful that as a soul sitter you can join me in this support. Hospice workers provide an invaluable service, one that is far outside our limited capabilities. They free us up as soul sitters to attend to the hearts of the dying and the living. Members of Hospice, from beginning to end, are caring and warm and provide a safe harbor for those of us navigating the stormy sea of the soul sitter. Because they are trained and innately gifted in their respective roles, they are in my opinion the single most important partner to families, patients, and soul sitters as we learn to bridge the life and death experience.

**The 5-Stages:** The 5-Stages as outlined by Elisabeth Kübler-Ross offer a wonderful resource for understanding the process of a terminally ill patient, or a patient facing the end of a long life. Remember to keep in mind they are not meant to imply that step one leads to step two, or three or four. Any one of the stages can be felt at random and fluctuate in and out of the person's life like the ocean's tide. It is important for the soul sitter's peace of mind to understand and have compassion for the process; not only for the person dying, but for yourself as well. Facing our mortality discharges many emotions that have been suppressed, maybe even for years.

Denial, anger, bargaining, depression, and or acceptance are human emotions that operate in our lives on a daily basis. Never more prevalent than when one is dealing with death, these emotions can become erratic, exaggerated and extreme. Awareness is the most powerful skill available to us in our lives. Becoming aware of the 5-Stages offers understanding during death's challenging process.

## A TRIAD FOR HERITAGE

- **Rituals**
- **Archiving and Memorials**
- **Positive Grief Method (PGM)**

**Valuing rituals.** Death, regardless of culture or geographical location, is processed by all humanity through ritual. Prior to the advent of plentiful hospitals and elder care facilities, most people died in their homes. After the death, more often than not, women attended to the body. They lovingly washed, dressed, and placed their loved one on display in a parlor. Friends and relatives would come to pay their respects and would follow the carriage or hearse to the cemetery where a service or committal was performed. In many traditions, people would talk to the open grave and toss a handful of dirt upon the coffin as an act of acknowledgment the departed was no longer with them. Judaism still practices this ritual.

Rituals are for the living and are invaluable in the emotional and mental healing of those left behind. Many religious traditions today no longer have "funerals" but instead have "celebrations of life" to acknowledge the valuable contribution the dying person left behind. Regardless of how your spiritual or local community shapes the ceremony, ceremonies provide a soft place to land for grieving families and friends. For many, this level of ritual can be enough; it can provide solace and peace as the final chapter spent with the deceased person comes to a close.

But for others, more may be required. In these cases, ritual is as varied as snowflakes. Perhaps a more personal ritual may be desired. The removal of taboos and/or fears around a more personal interaction with the deceased would go a long way in helping heal the sadness and the finality of death. Any ritual beyond the traditional is a very personal choice and if it is within reason (and sanity) should be encouraged. We all, each of us, have personal needs when it comes to processing our own emotions around death. But if someone finds they need more, their needs should be considered. My own personal experience with this was when Mom gave me permission to attend to Grandma Green at the mortuary.

Some examples of ritual could be simply sitting with the loved one, immediately following death, and talking to the person, even holding a hand or showing affection via a hug or kiss on the cheek. Other rituals might include:

* Bathing the deceased and tending to their hair and clothing
* Holding hands, have someone lead the aggrieved in a prayer

*    Taking a snippet of hair to keep in a locket or safe place
*    Reading a spiritual or Biblical verse aloud
*    Praying or sitting in silence with them
*    Listing the many ways you are grateful to them for their life
*    Giving yourself permission to be comforted by another

These are only ideas and perhaps you or the person(s) you are soul sitting will have their own personal ritual that would be meaningful to them. The whole idea is to support the value of ritual and not make ritual's voice wrong or morbid. It is how humankind has healed and traversed the reality of death for millennia. It is the song we sing with the Universe, in our sorrow, our gratitude, and our longing to know there is more.

You will, if you are paying attention, see that we are surrounded every day with ritual. We experience it in baptisms, in weddings, in anniversary and birthdays, even in how we set the table or put a child to bed at night. Encourage the people you soul sit for (should the opportunity present itself) to engage in ritual, not only at death's arrival, but for all the days in between. You can advocate to the dying person a ritual that will leave a legacy for their loved ones. One mother quilted for the grandchildren who would only know her through her pictures. Others record their thoughts and remembrances. A ritual can be created between the family members and the dying person, with permission of the person dying.

As a soul sitter, you can practice ritual through a prayer, recording journal entries, or playing music. Ritual is simply the act of creating precious memories that will last for years to come. Death is part of life's circle and the use of ritual is a healing tool all of us can use in our toolbox.

**Archiving Life:** The life we live, regardless of its contents, should not be wasted. All life is a bit messy; living it is an imperfect act. While none of us are without skeletons in our closets, there is also the gift of a life lived that has tremendous value. Our personal book is filled with stories and events that not only shape us, but also shape our loved ones, our friends, and even strangers to some degree. I am not suggesting a "tell all" book about stories from the closets of life. However, there is great value in sharing the highs and the lows, the challenges and the victories that flavor a person's life experience. I think we can all agree that life is, at its very best, challenging to live…even when we love our life and all it represents. Someone once said 'Our life begins with an open parenthesis and ends with a closed one. It is the stuff between that really matters.' But to remove the parentheses, to separate life from death, is like trying to separate a flower from its stem. It cannot be done, for if separated, it is not representative of the whole. Every moment, regardless of its high or low, offers a gift to us and it is our responsibility to open that gift.

The person who has died has left a legacy, good, bad, or indifferent. Many packages of that person's life remain unopened, waiting for our eager hearts and hands to open those gifts. As soul sitters, we can help the grieved (if they choose to) to slowly pick up those unopened packages and make the gifts personal and their own. In what sometimes feels like the battlefield called "ends" or "deaths," our <u>real need</u> comes forward like a valiant soldier who has fought long and hard. That real need is our need to be heard. Sadly, most of us wait all our lives for that gift. Sometimes we talk so much, there is never room for listening.

But endings, our final days, always offer a sacred space for this to happen.

Perhaps you can take notes or record conversations with the person who is about to die. As a soul sitter, you can also encourage friends and family to share stories about their passing loved one and how that person impacted or left their thumbprint on life. Whether it is written, recorded, or simply heard, there is great healing and power that comes from the parenthetical, multi-chaptered life we live.

**Create a Memorial:** Washington D.C. is a remarkable example of remembering the deceased through memorial. As you travel along the beltway, you can see the many iconic buildings of our American heritage. The Lincoln memorial at one end of the Mall, the Washington Monument at the opposite end; the White House surrounded by the Jefferson Memorial and Capitol Building; the Vietnam Memorial and the Holocaust Museum all represent memorials, on a grand scale, that honor those who have died.

Honoring the people we love brings us comfort. Soul sitters can urge or encourage loved ones of the departed to create their own memorials. It can be created in one of many ways, not limiting ourselves to solely creating a headstone on a cemetery plot. It does not have to be expensive or even expansive, it is simply important to give yourself permission to memorialize a loved one with something personal and significant to you. It can be as simple as a scrap book, planting rosemary (a commonly recognized symbol for remembrance), a tree or rose bush in your yard, or hanging a memorable picture on a wall. Some families create fundraising events to find a cure or to raise awareness for a disease or create a memorial scholarship fund, while those with resources may build a wing to a hospital. Each idea has equal value if it offers you a way to say "thank you" for a life well lived. No one idea is too small or too large for that matter.. It is another tool that can be employed as we set sail on the sea of our own life.

**Positive Grief Method:** In Chapter Four, the Positive Grief Method (PGM) was introduced as a way to process your emotions (or your loved one's emotions) around the experience of death. The simple but powerful ideas presented cannot be underestimated for their value. Ceremonies are a PGM that has been used for millennia to help heal broken hearts, broken dreams, and broken lives. Ceremonies are a way of recording life. Symbolically, through ceremony, we bridge our emotions back to life experiences in a way that allows us to be present and move forward. Experiencing death is a highly charged emotional experience. Loss is real and leaves a void, unless we know how to anchor that loss in the ongoing life we are asked to continue living. I invite you to make whatever ceremonies you choose to create personal, so your heart can have a soft place to land…and so you can find comfort in them when you feel lost.

## A POSTSCRIPT

I want to acknowledge each reader for even considering becoming or acting as a soul sitter. It is no easy or small task. It asks a great deal of us and in the process, it is critical that, while we are selfless, we also take care of our own emotional needs around loss. Many soul sitters will be working in hospitals or hospices, but for the most part, as I have already stated, will be infrequent practitioners. For most soul sitters, you come from a larger humanistic pool of regular, caring people who simply wish to reach out to family and friends in a time of need. Please, never take your own spiritual and emotional stamina for granted. You will be hearing, and even absorbing, many painful things and will need your own special brand of love and care.

Caring for the dying is a noble, loving act. It is also exhausting. As a soul sitter, there may be experiences or moments when sharing your emotional pain with those you are caring for might be detrimental to each of you. As someone caring for a terminally ill friend or family member, your own emotions will be fragile. It is important to be honest and show your feelings in tender moments. There are no set rules because everyone's experience is very different.

As you encourage, coach, and guide others throughout the days preceding death, sharing your fears is acceptable and necessary; but it is important to share them with an objective person, someone you feel safe with **outside** of the one who is passing and his or her family. Anyone, at any stage of life, might qualify as a soul sitter. If you have found yourself in that role, allow yourself the gift of a separate support system. Once you know you will be doing this, it is important to your own well-being to put into place someone you can turn to for emotional and spiritual nourishment and support. Whether through conversation with another person or finding inspiration and strength through literature, soul sitters **<u>absolutely</u>** need to find a way to take care of their own sense of loss and grief as they embark on the path of caring for others.

## THE SOUL SITTER'S STOOL
## TRIADS OF SOUL CARE

Triad for Intuitive Care
- Learn to empty self
- Move beyond clichés when helping people
- Relate to all people based on the five Bridge Steps

Triad for Advocacy
- Be an advocate
- Be an advocate for Palliative & Hospice care
- Understand Kübler-Ross' 5-Stages

Triad for Heritage
- Value rituals
- Archive and create memorials
- Practice the Positive Grief Method (PGM)

# Chapter Six
# Using a Full Deck

*A question asked in the right way often points to
its own answer.*

EDWARD HODNETT

It is never easy to create conversation with those who are
close to the end of their life. Where we are accustomed to
talking about the weather or our summer vacation plans, those
kinds of conversations become trivial at the end of someone's
life. It has been my experience that when I am confronted with
the unfamiliar, my brain freezes. Thoughtful conversation can
become locked away when we stare into the eyes of those who
know they are dying. Intellectually, I know they are dying. Others
in the room have accepted this as true. Yet, words escape us when
it comes to the last days with our loved ones. We are trying to
suppress our own fears on one hand, and on the other, we just
don't know what to say.

As I have grown in my experience with soul sitting, I continue
to be graced with inspiration I can only attribute to my Mother
Guides. As I became aware of the discomfort some people had
while visiting their loved one, I received a wonderful idea that

became what I call the Miracle Dialogue Deck. It is made up of different topics and questions for family members and friends to ask their loved ones in their final days. The Miracle Dialogue Deck serves a dual purpose. First, it offers your loved ones an opportunity to share little known things about themselves with you. Secondly, it offers family members an opportunity to talk with each other.

To demonstrate how this has worked, I would like to share a personal story with you. My brother Shane's wife, Lori, used them when her step-father, Jerry, was nearing the end of his life and entered the care of San Diego Hospice. He was admitted into a 24-bed facility that was designed more like a peaceful resort than a hospital. Since Jerry was someone who had thoroughly enjoyed celebrations for life's many blessings, his loving family turned his room into a party. Jerry was grateful and appreciated being surrounding by his family. He was unable to easily join in with the conversations in the room because of the oxygen mask. Otherwise alert, he saw everything they had done for him…the cake and the balloons, the grandchildren and his family.

One evening, with his grandchildren gathered around him, his daughter drew a card from the deck. Jerry was in and out of consciousness, and the room had become quiet when she asked the question, "When you were a kid, what was your favorite movie?" Suddenly, Jerry's eyes got big, and he said, "Hopalong Cassidy." The family was thrilled to have his response and drew another card. This time, they asked him who is favorite actor was. Everyone assumed they knew it was John Wayne. To their surprise and delight, he responded with Dean Martin. It was a small and interesting thing to learn at the end of life, and the family had a new and endearing insight into their dad and granddad.

I believe this simple story has tremendous value. First and foremost, it taught me that the person who is dying is often very present in the room, whether you realize it or not. Even people in a coma, once conscious, have reported hearing conversations that occurred while they were unconscious. It is of tremendous value to recognize that our spirit is present, even though our body is failing. Jerry was able to participate and teach us that by his example. Secondly, we can continue to learn from our loved ones even upon their death beds. There is often so little known about the person. We assume so much based upon our perceptions. And unfortunately, many times we never give ourselves a chance to really know someone.

The Miracle Dialogue Deck will help you fill the communication gap. Filled with beautiful, fun and sometimes insightful questions, it will also help you discover special memories that may comfort you on those nights when you feel the absence of your loved one. Using the deck of questions will allow you to know them better and discover the things that brought them joy. For Jerry's family, it created a memory in his last days.

The Miracle Dialogue Deck also offers a way to demonstrate your gratitude. When we open up dialogue with another person, we make deeper and longer lasting connections to them, regardless of their physical presence. People will feel more valued because you cared to ask about them and they will know they are leaving a legacy. In the end, the most valuable thing we can say to anyone is "thank you." When we can do this, we are saying so much more: "I'm glad you were born," or "Thank you for your good example in life," or "Your presence mattered to me."

You do not have to have a history of getting along fabulously with a person to show this kind of appreciation. It is something that emerges from the human spirit. There have been a couple of people in my life with whom I had some lingering estrangement, but I was able to look at them on their deathbed and say, "Thank you. I know we had some rough times, but I am glad you were part of my life. You mattered." Through the power of appreciation you may even realize the lesson that person was there to teach you through your estrangement.

For a free digital download of the Miracle Dialogue Deck, please visit the Soul Sitter website at www.soulsitter.com.

# Chapter Seven
# Spiritual Silence

*We need to find God, and he cannot be found in noise and restlessness.*

*God is the friend of silence. See how nature - trees, flowers, grass- grows in silence;*

*see the stars, the moon and the sun, how they move in silence...*

*We need silence to be able to touch souls.*

MOTHER THERESA

My godmother, Mary, taught me many things as I walked the pathway with her that was leading to her own death. She had been a practicing Catholic for many years who, at some point in her life, had given herself permission to explore her spirituality, which also included the mysticism practiced by Native Americans. Her path to her own spiritual foundation inspired me to return to the roots I had planted as a young girl in the Catholic Church. I will always feel the deep resonance of Christ's message and the reassurance that I discovered waiting for me in my renewed devotion.

It is not my intention to offer a treatise or to appear to be an expert on the subject of spirituality or religion. But in the course of being a soul sitter, most people (when faced with the reality of mortality) will come face to face with their personal relationship with their idea of God or a greater Being by any other name. This chapter is intended not as a spiritual discourse or lecture, but will provide some guidelines if or when this may occur.

**When the person dying decides to join a religious organization**

As a side benefit of writing this book, my family's memory bank has been jogged and many wonderful stories have surfaced about our beloved relatives. One that I had forgotten was the story about my dad's mother, Grandma Green. As I have described her, Grandma Green was a self-proclaimed bawdy woman who fought the concepts of the Catholic Church while she lived. Her husband and son were practicing Catholics. But in the last days of her life, she decided to convert. I honestly cannot tell you why. I can only assume that she either decided she was wrong or didn't want to take any chances! Either way, she beseeched Dad to talk to the priest to convert her, also giving her the grace of the last rites at death to be performed by the church priest. As my father had honored his mother for all of her life, this one last request was easy for him. A priest came and baptized Grandma Green.

As a Catholic, the rights of communion are given to those who are baptized into the faith. Grandma Green was to receive her communion (the Eucharist) weekly. Our pastor, however was not always available. So he conferred upon Dad the rights to present communion for his mom. I think that Dad was thrilled to play this honorable role for his mother.

When the first Sunday arrived for Dad to offer her communion, the family gathered around Grandma Green's bed. Dad, by this time was extremely nervous and, like all good sons, wanted to administer the Eucharist perfectly. (For those who are unfamiliar with the Catholic communion, as the priest presents the wafer to the congregant he says, "The body of Christ.") When he got to his line and offered the Eucharist to Grandma Green, his nerves got the best of him. In retrospect, I am sure he was shaking in his cowboy boots a little! As poised as he could be, instead of the standard blessing, he accidentally said, "In God We Trust." No one caught this faux-pas but Mom. But looking back, it was the perfect thing to say to his mom who was unfamiliar with the meaning of the pastor's words.

The lesson I learned from this and other personal experiences has served me as a soul sitter. If, for any reason, something of this nature is requested by the dying person, encourage and support it. It does not have to be perfect or precise. It simply needs to be conveyed in a way that feels authentic and real to the person dying. Just honor any dying wish. Certainly, follow the precepts of the faith the dying person is being initiated into, if the wish is a religious conversion, but don't let the need of perfectionism dilute the intent. Grandma Green, according to the Catholic guidelines, had been received into the arms of its faith. And Grandma Green accepted it for indeed, at this point, she did trust in God!

## When the person dying or a loved one turns away from their faith

This can be painful to witness, regardless of your spiritual or religious persuasion; or whether you believe in a God. If the person, up until this time has been devout, it may feel foreign to you. Something of their persona has slipped away. Perhaps even something you admired about them even if you did not agree with their personal choices. If this happens, it is most likely the person is feeling betrayed by his or her faith. For the family or friends who have not strayed from their faith, this can be especially disarming. Fears could arise for you or for them based upon their belief in the afterlife.

Feelings of betrayal when being faced with death, especially if it is untimely, will challenge even the most holy of human beings. Even Mother Theresa's faith was shaken at times as she faced death on a daily basis. If you are the observer, watching your loved one turn away from a former faith or belief, there are a couple of things you can do. One, you can seek counsel from your pastor; or two, you can seek the love and support from a friend or prayer circle. I have heard it said that it is okay if you don't believe in God, God still believes in you. For those who worry about the fate of their loved one, it is not your role to judge. The only thing available to you is to enter into your own silence, into your own prayer and faith. By example and demonstration, the simple act of acceptance may bring peace to the situation.

However, this is a time to hand over your fears and concerns to your own faith and seek comfort and counsel from someone who is an expert in this area. In the end, kindness is the only thing that matters.

Hospice has professionally trained spiritual counselors and pastors who work with families every day. Seek out their services or the counsel of someone you trust. Sometimes a psychologist or other mental health professional can guide you to a safe place to explore possibilities. I would only advise that any formal action (such as joining a different faith) be delayed until your anguish has passed. Your path will always be available to you later. The solace received if this is a true need can buoy you with strength and peace. There are avenues to walk down, hands to hold, and people who care. If you truly desire this for yourself, it only takes your willingness. There is a beautiful Buddhist proverb that says, "When the student is ready, the teacher will appear." It has become a common saying, but I think it is important to recognize it came from ancient wisdom. Willingness is the soul's breath.

There is a value for soul sitters in having a spiritual connection. While great debates continue around our globe over which path is the "right" path, I offer these thoughts because I know many arrive at death's door (either their own or in the face of losing someone we love) seeking to understand life's meaning. Death cannot be unwoven from life any more than our hearts can stand separately from our body. The feeling of connection we have when we are with our loved ones, and the cavity that is left when they are no longer living, can only be filled with the intangible-tangible. Some call it God, others call it science, and still others call it Universe or a Higher Power. A rose by any other name would smell as sweet, as Shakespeare brilliantly reminded us.

## A POSTSCRIPT

As you begin this journey, I hope my story enables you to embrace the idea that all endings birth new beginnings. I am one of a silent majority who has received messages from their loved ones who have passed away. If you have had a similar experience, I want to reassure you that you are not crazy. If you have not had these experiences, allow yourself to consider (if only for a moment) there is but a thin veil between this life and the other side. The past two years has taught me that life is endless and we are but a child of that endlessness. Because a story ends, it does not mean it ceases to exist. Our memories, at any moment in time, can be the unbroken circle of our loved one's life's signature.

I am deeply hopeful our readers find a way to come to terms with the reality that death is part of life. At the same time, I am equally hopeful that by embracing death, we will be able to embrace our own lives with more passion and conviction.

I want to encourage you to ask for guidance. You will feel less isolated, less lonely if you reach out to your higher power. My journey since Miraval has taken me down many new pathways. Those who support Soul Sitters go forward with our work, prayerfully asking that our acts be based in humility, that our hearts are loving and compassionate, and our minds open and receptive to changing and evolving ideas.

The Soul Sitter Creed is to listen at all times, to the people who come searching and to the whisper of the Divine (or our higher power) as well. We dedicate ourselves to be active listeners, patient and kind by example. Recognizing we are all spiritual beings having a human experience, we make allowances for our humanity and our flaws. Our intention is to offer insight, share guidance, and help others find balance as they face the ultimate test of life. We wish Soul Sitters to be a flashlight on a dark journey. We don't need to see the end of the unfamiliar road; we only need to be mindful of the next step.

# Chapter Eight
# The Purposeful Passage

*Do the difficult things while they are easy to do*
*the great things while they are small.*
*A journey of a thousand miles must begin with a single step.*

LAO TZU

Soul sitting is something that can begin with us. To be truthful, it should begin with us, individually, while we have the presence of mind (and the emotional and mental clarity) necessary to face such a crucial time in our own lives. Now that you have embraced the concept of the Soul Sitter, you are in a unique position to create a purposeful passage so you can live a more purposeful life.

The five separate times I have cared for my dying loved ones created fertile ground and gave me pause to consider my own death. I began asking serious questions of my own life and its ending. While I understood that I, perhaps, had no way to predict the time or circumstances of my death, what I might be able to do was inform those I loved of what was important to me. I realized I wanted to equip and comfort my family without leaving them second guessing as to what I wanted or what they should do.

Too often, families are torn apart when facing the many decisions to be made regarding the death of a loved one. The death of a mother, a father, or even siblings, when left to interpretation or supposition, creates often stressful or even tragic results. One surviving person wants one thing during the illness or after the person has died, while another wishes for a different result or experience. One child believes their parent wanted one thing, while the other child may have knowledge of a different outcome desired by the parent.

I don't believe this is something that happens on purpose. In a world where "fast forward" seems to be the life-train we all ride on, I have found that few plan for their death or make an attempt to script the circumstances for the end of life.

Confusion does not confine itself to the surviving spouse, children, or siblings...or even friends. It can also cloud the ability of those who are dying to ask for what they want. Many of us are not used to being cared for and/or receiving care and/or help from others. At the end of our life, most of us have no other choice. There comes a time for most when surrender is the only option and accepting help the only answer.

When my mother-in-law Edna was in our home during the final days of her life, she shared with me that she felt like a burden. She was anxious about <u>being</u> a burden and continually acquiesced to my own style of caregiving/soul sitting. She was dear and sweet and her desire was to be as little a burden as possible, while all I wanted to do was serve and care for her in whatever capacity had meaning for her. I wanted to do whatever I could to make her final days meaningful. And while I believe I made the end of her life better, I sadly never considered asking her what might be really important to **her**, until long after she passed away. At the time of caring for her, I had no tools to ease the guilt she seemed to be carrying in her heart. Truthfully, there probably was not a way since she had never made her wishes known to anyone.

As I developed Soul Sitters, the idea of Edna's guilty feelings about my caring for her in the final days of her life haunted me. At the time of her death, I desperately wanted to reassure her, to ease her emotional guilt. I have no idea if the things I did were things she wanted. The more I considered this (and the more people shared their personal stories with me through Soul Sitters), the more acutely aware I became of the importance of communicating our individual wishes to our families. We create a Will for the things in our life; why not create a spiritual and emotional Will to help others know how they can best serve us? We all needed a protocol, a plan. We all needed a passage plan.

When I finally realized how simple the solution was, I was deeply relieved. Just the idea of creating a passage plan, before I had even considered what it might look like, eased any anxiety I had ever felt about my own death. I saw it as a simple way to offer solace and comfort to my family. If they knew what was important to me then they no longer had to be involved in making these important decisions on my behalf. They could simply spend my final days with me, in peace, without worrying about whether they were doing what I wanted. I knew this would be especially true if I was in a coma.

I understand that right now you may be physically well and your own death is the last thing on your mind. You may still be hurting and grieving the loss of your loved one. Everything in life is timing. But timing only matters when we are aware of answers and solutions. I understand that even thinking about tomorrow, right now, may be a bit of stretch for you. But, there may come a time when you are ready to consider how you would like your own final days to look.

Creating a passage plan is something all of us can do. When I created my own passage plan, it made living my life a richer experience. I began to appreciate the many events of my life, even the hard times. It became obvious: how I managed or mastered each event would make up the days of the rest of my life. I wanted to make each day count.

If you are wondering to yourself, "Would creating a passage plan make a difference in my life?" I can only share with you that it will. Perhaps there were challenges you faced when going through the death of your loved one and you simply do not wish your children or family to experience unnecessary road bumps similar to those you may have just encountered. Or maybe, you simply want to make a very difficult and heartbreaking time less stressful. If so, please consider the following:

* Would you like to equip and comfort your loved ones emotionally and spiritually at the time of your death?
* Would putting your wishes down on paper help relieve stress for your family?
* Would you like to help those caring for you at the end of your life feel more assured they are doing the right thing?

* Would you like to leave a legacy of harmonious passing for your family, knowing they are at peace for having provided things of importance to you along the way?
* Would having a say over your own final days offer you peace of mind?
* Would you like your medical team to know the things that are personally important to you? (Maybe Mozart in the operating room...)
* Would you like to dispel any disagreements your surviving family members might have regarding your wishes?

Having a passage plan could be the perfect handoff as you pass on this book to your loved ones. I think back on my time with my grandmothers, my dad, my mother-in-law and Godmother. They each taught me something of importance when it came to the end of their lives. The most treasured gifts I gleamed from them were: 1) the importance of communication to my family and 2) the nature and value of every precious moment I spent with them as they neared their final breath.

If your loved one is still with you and you find yourself in the process of soul sitting, I encourage you to ask your loved one any one of a hundred questions that will help you help them. There is no time to waste and the answers that come will offer you clarity and surety. This is not the time for timidity but for a strong courageous heart. If you ask your questions sincerely, with an intention to serve, you will both win. For more information, or if you would like help creating your own passage plan (or need a guideline that will help you open this conversation between you and your loved one), please see the information provided at the back of this book.

~ ~ ~ ~ ~ ~ ~ ~ ~ ~ ~ ~ ~

I wish you well in your life. I wish you, more than anything, peace. It is my deepest hope that my inspired work relieves the burden of your heart (if only for a moment). You have my sincerest sympathy for the loss you have experienced or will in the near future. I can only reassure you that time will heal the acuteness of the pain. And I can also reassure you that your loved one will remain in your heart forever.

# Epilogue

*In my end is my beginning.*

T.S. ELIOT

I have been on a steep learning curve as Soul Sitters has unveiled itself over the past year. Some of the revelations have been challenging. One is that all good things are worth waiting for. The other is that any road I travel is worth traveling upon when it is headed in the right direction. It began with an innocent business trip, wanting nothing more than to make smart business connections that would support my career. What it ended up being was a life-changing event — not because of the things that happened, but because I chose to act on what happened. It was an ending for me, an ending of a lifestyle and a perspective that was limited in its scope. It was also my beginning.

From the experience I had with my dying relatives, especially the "miracles" that came to me after they had passed; to my experience soul sitting my Godmother, Mary, as she approached her death, until her presence communicated to me that early morning in Arizona; to the many conversations I have had with others since I began this work — one thing is vividly apparent. Our lives do not end when our bodies die. The many promises I heard as a young Catholic girl and the goose bump experiences since have spoken to the promise of many masters who have walked on this Earth — that our souls are eternal and our mystical heart does indeed beat forever.

Death is a phenomenon of life, the integrated piece of living as a human being (or any being) on planet Earth. It is the single shared experience of all life; there is a beginning, middle, and an end. In the same way our breath cannot be separated from our lungs but only passed through, so life breathes in and nourishes our body until our body says "no more." Death is a tremendously sacred moment, a time when the period at the end of the sentence feels so concrete. But as we are able to reframe our definition and/or perception of death, our experience with it changes. What feels like an "end" can become a validation of life that makes every moment sweeter and more precious. Sogyal Rinpoche in his book *The Tibetan Book of Living and Dying* reflects on the fear that colors many Western cultures. As a Tibetan monk, he learned that death is the next phase of our soul's experience, something to be honored and cherished. It is not to be feared, although it certainly can and should be grieved. With much insight, he reflected:

> *"What all of this is showing us, with painful clarity, is that now more than ever before, we need a fundamental change in our attitude toward death and dying."*

As a soul sitter, you have the opportunity to reframe how you feel about this process, using the tools and concepts inspired and whispered to me and that I now share with you. Most of you reading this book will be doing so because you have found yourself in the midst of a situation you were ill prepared for. To those, I am deeply hopeful that the methodologies found in these pages will serve the urgent need for which you are trying to find solutions.

It is my genuine hope, however, that this opens a dialogue around death and dying and moves us closer and closer to everyday and practical acceptance of the circle of life that begins with our first breath and culminates in our last. There is no guarantee that even having the tools will give you a full measure of ease that will buffer your shock, especially when death is sudden. But again, it can and God willing it will, open up conversations that will change how we see death.

If there was an intention or wish I have, it would be for every soul sitter, whether by career choice or by circumstance, to find relief, peace within their hearts, and a soft place to land when confronted with the act of soul sitting. In truth, we soul sit each other every day, in some way, either by example or through support of our friends and family. I wish for my story and the many systems handed to me from a much wiser place than my own imagination, to serve you as you walk through the days, weeks, months, and years of your life.

Be kind to yourself; be kind to others. Learn to listen with an open heart, absent any agendas, prejudices, or judgments. If an end of a relationship is inevitable, let it end with grace and dignity for everyone. Endings are seasons in our life and to hate them, deny them, or resent them is a waste of the very gift of breath we all receive, regardless of how we live or who we are.

Life gives us the opportunity to practice our response to death with every passing moment. Do not take lightly the idea that "this too shall pass" for EVERYTHING does, with or without our permission. No amount of positive thinking can prevent death from happening, it can only postpone it. But mindfulness and prayer powerfully change us. In death is the nature of being alive. And being alive is our gift. Thank you for allowing me into your heart and your life, to share my story and to perhaps offer you solace in a time of great need. It has been my honor. It is now my life's work, and it will forever be my heart's treasure.

# A Message from Candace

When I was reintroduced to Stacey Canfield, (we had met eleven years prior to our reunion) I had no idea that our meeting would be my own turning point. She had made the decision to redesign her first edition of Soul Sitters and I volunteered to offer feedback and assistance to the process. What it became was so much more. In Stacey, I feel I have discovered a long-lost soul sister and dear friend; through Soul Sitters, I found my purpose and direction.

From the very beginning of our journey together, I understood her intent and her desired outcome for the book. Her story was deeply moving; her experiences felt familiar and authentic. Like her, my experiences with the death of family and others had taught me that life is endless and that my loved ones were closer to me than I could imagine or logically explain. I had experienced the presence of my beloved mother who had passed away, the presence of my father the morning he died, and other mystical experiences around death. I knew, because of my experiences, that we do not "die" as we perceive death but that we only shed the body. Even ten years after her death, I still feel my mother's presence and guidance. I hear her soft spoken words of advice as I traverse the many moments, challenges, and experiences of my own life. She has never left my side.

I believe in Stacey's goal: to introduce a new language for death to our Western culture. I have continued to appreciate that death is the one thing (regardless of your culture, religion, belief, or lifestyle) that we all share. I feel deep tolerance for other people's challenges and flaws — perhaps because I know I have been, at some point in time, the beggar and thief or the queen or ruler, and all things in between. Our lives are meant to be experienced from a deep and sacred perspective, and as I continue to open to new perspectives, I find peace and purpose in everything.

I am grateful to Stacey for trusting me, for passing her "child" in the form of Soul Sitters into my care. I treasure that she was willing to be open and transparent as we have re-approached her story and the telling of it. It was an honor to give her voice back to her story. It was easy to validate her heart, her voice, and her experience in a way that only increased my own faith and determination. With Stacey, I too found my voice and my purpose. I am hopeful that everyone who takes time to read *The Soul Sitter's Handbook* finds incredible priceless value, not just in the words but in the message between the lines. It can, by your permission and your permission alone, shift your own life into a deeper and more meaningful place. Perhaps you may even discover a clear space within your heart for peace in your (and your beloved families' and friends') life process.

Wishing you wisdom and courage as you enter the world of soul sitting; after all, in the end, we are all soul sitters to each other. Namasté.

*Candace Conradi*

As shared in Chapter Eight:
A Purposeful Passage:

# My Gift to You!

A comprehensive blueprint to equip and comfort
your loved ones at your passing.

# The PASSAGE PLAN

Plan what you want to support you
physically, emotionally and spiritually.

*The Passage Plan was inspired by and dedicated
to my mother-in-law, Edna Canfield.
Thank you Edna for allowing us to be your
Soul Sitters.*

Pictured: Son Daniel and his mother, Edna Canfield
December 1, 2003

Download your free copy of The Passage Plan at
**www.soulsitters.com/passageplan**

Join our Soul Sitter community at
**www.soulsitters.com**
and recieve a free monthly newsletter
The Soul Sitters *Journal*

Sitters

A comforting community for those
facing the loss of a loved one

As mentioned in Chapter 6,
The MIRACLE DIALOGUE DECK opens the door to a
wonderful time of sharing.

# DOWNLOAD A FREE TRIAL SET TODAY!

*VISIT*
*www.soulsitters.com/dialogue-deck.*
*and receive 10 cards with 30 easy questions for free!*

## The MIRACLE DIALOGUE DECK
### is designed to:

- Encourage meaningful conversations through the gift of positive thoughts and memories.

- Spark easy and lighthearted communication with family and friends.

- Create an heirloom legacy of little known facts about your loved one.

- Be fun, simple and easy to use, even by children.

*DOWNLOAD AND PRINT ON ANY COMPUTER START YOUR*
*OWN "MIRACLE OF DIALOGUE" TODAY*

CPSIA information can be obtained at www.ICGtesting.com
Printed in the USA
BVOW011642130912

300239BV00001B/3/P